1001

WAYS TO

STAY YOUNG

NATURALLY

Susannah Marriott

LONDON, NEW YORK, MUNICH,
MELBOURNE, DELHI

For Lyn, Jo, Mary, Anna, Sue, Nicoletta, Georgia, Stacey, Charlotte,
Rosie and Rachel

Project editor Angela Baynham
Project art editor Carole Ash at Project 360
Senior editor Esther Ripley
Senior art editor Peggy Sadler
Photographer Ruth Jenkinson
DTP designer Sonia Charbonnier
Production controller Clare McLean
Managing editor Penny Warren
Managing art editor Marianne Markham
Jacket designer Vicky Read
Jacket editor Adam Powley
Publishing director Corinne Roberts
Yoga tips Amanda Brown
Homeopathic/herbal tips Julia Linfoot BSc MCPH MAI

Caution: if you are pregnant or have a medical condition, do not use herbs
(including herbal teas) without consulting a qualified herbal practitioner.
Similarly, some oils should not be used if you are pregnant or breastfeeding, or
if you have high blood pressure, kidney problems, or epilepsy. When using oils,
take note of the manufacturer's cautions and those on tips and recipes and never
use more drops than is recommended. Avoid body masks, scrubs, very hot and
salt baths during pregnancy. The advice and information on health matters
given in this book is not intended as a substitute for qualified medical advice
and neither the publisher not the author accept any legal responsibility for
personal injury, or damage, or loss arising from its use or misuse.

First published in Great Britain in 2007
by Dorling Kindersley Limited, 80 Strand, London WC2R ORL
A Penguin Company

ISBN: 978-1-4053-1761-0

Reproduced by GRB, Italy
Printed and bound by Sheck Wah Tong, China

Discover more at
www.dk.com

Contents

Introduction

We are the generations who are determined to stay young forever. Whether you were part of the youth movements that created Woodstock and the Glastonbury festival, punk rock and rave culture, hip hop and the first and second summers of love or are simply facing up to your first grey hairs and wondering how to live a greener life, you probably feel as I do. How can we possibly grow old? Our role models are still living the life – writing classic tunes, designing show-stopping collections, becoming the face of global cosmetics companies – so why shouldn't we?

We have fought to do it our way. Believing individuals could make a difference, we campaigned for women's and gay rights and against wars and the establishment. A worldwide study suggests this makes us more likely to be sexually satisfied into our 80s and beyond. Our embracing of eco culture – it was us folks who fought to ban the bomb, declared meat is murder and founded Greenpeace – means we demand that our youth-enhancing beauty products and foods be ethical and green. Recent years have seen a big change in attitude to ageing and we can all benefit – we no longer have to grow old to order. Forty is now considered to be no age at all; 50 could be the new 40, and 60 is the time of your life.

This book is packed with tips to keep us having it all as we move through the decades: how to eat well and defy ageing through nutrition; how to build exercise into life to boost energy and beat fatigue; recipes for organic wrinkle erasers and non-toxic cleaners; quick ways to bat away stress, beat insomnia; and how to keep the heart, brain, bones and joints working well so we look good and feel great forever.

As individuals, making small differences to lifestyle not only enhances wellbeing, it may increase lifespan. In a recent survey by Cambridge University of people aged over 45, simply eating a single apple or pear every day seemed to equate with an extra two years of life. Not smoking added five years; moderate exercise and eating five portions of fruit and veg a day three more each.

Lifestyle changes don't have to entail deprivation to have an impact on longevity. And often they come in the form of treats – a glass of wine and a little fine dark chocolate, a lunchtime massage, sociable nights out and a funny movie may add years to our lives as well as life to our years.

Since 1994, the New England Centenarian Study has been monitoring people who live to at least 100 to discover the secrets of successful ageing. In doing so, it has disproved the theory that the older we grow, the sicker we become. To the contrary, it reveals that the older we get, the healthier we have been. Seventy five per cent of centenarians live independently to the age of 96. Factors they share include a lean body, years without smoking, destressing skills, and a history of giving birth after 35 (birth after 40 equates with a four times greater chance of living to 100!). And, of course, good genes. The secret might be to take the advice of the principal investigator for the study, Dr Thomas Perls: instead of wondering how to stay young, we should think about how to age well. Here are 1001 tips to start us off.

Susannah Marriott

Susannah Marriott   Cornwall 2007

1 Eating naturally

Take a natural approach to food and enjoy the gourmand experience. A diet that benefits the heart and keeps the brain youthful encourages you to add variety to your plate – to feast on ripe fruit and vegetables, herbs and spices, and to luxuriate in the taste of well-raised meat and wild fish bought fresh and prepared simply. Natural foods contain a startling number of anti-ageing ingredients. These include heart-friendly fats, protective plant substances and youth-preserving antioxidants that can neutralize free radicals – the unstable molecules that kickstart the body's ageing processes prematurely and are increased in the body by exposure to stress, pollution, UV rays, cigarette smoke and unhealthy fats.

Natural nutrition

Eating food in as close to its natural state as possible helps ensure maximum exposure to youth-enhancing nutrients, many of which are lost during storage, processing and cooking. It also reduces your exposure to artificial additives used to enhance the flavour, texture, colour and shelf-life of processed foods, from ready meals to diet dishes.

Eat unprocessed seasonal fruit to make the most of its anti-ageing properties.

1
Five a day
Keep looking and feeling young and help ward off diseases of ageing, from Alzheimer's to stroke and heart disease, by eating more fruit and vegetables. They are rich in antioxidants, and the biologically active ingredients of plant pigments and flavourings have anti-ageing properties, too. Aim to eat a minimum of five portions of fruit and vegetables daily – and up to nine if you can.

2
Fitting in fruit
To boost the number of fruit servings you eat each day, slice fresh fruit or spoon soaked dried fruit onto morning muesli. Snack on grapes, dried fruit and berries, and eat an apple or banana mid-morning or afternoon. Follow meals with a fruit salad, baked or poached fruit, or treat yourself to pieces of fruit dipped in fine dark melted chocolate.

3
Colour combos
A rainbow of colours on the plate ensures you are getting a good intake of plant chemicals. Naturally deep green, yellow and red foods contain antioxidant carotenoids that boost immunity and offer protection against heart disease, cancer, DNA damage and age-related sight problems. Include peppers, broccoli, spinach, sweet potatoes, carrots and pumpkin in your diet, plus extra-virgin olive oil to aid absorption.

4
Fresh is best
Choose ripe, seasonal fruit and vegetables and grains in their whole form to ensure maximum flavour while retaining vitamins and

minerals, antioxidant compounds and other plant nutrients which are destroyed by processing.

5
Grow your own
The best way to ensure the freshest, most flavourful organic fruit and vegetables is to grow them yourself. Even a city balcony can provide a good supply of tomatoes, salad leaves, herbs and soft fruit.

6
Increasing variety
Diversity is the key to a healthy diet, since no one food can provide all the nutrients and antioxidants the body needs. Be adventurous and introduce new foods when you can.

7
Think like a vegetarian

Plant foods contain such life-enhancing properties that long-term vegetarians are 20 per cent less likely to die prematurely than meat eaters. You don't have to become a vegetarian to reap the benefits. Serve meals with two or three vegetables and salads on the side, and add extra vegetables to dishes such as stir-fries, casseroles and soups.

8
Resensitize your tastebuds

If your diet majors on slimming foods and processed meals, you might be amazed by the taste of fresh produce. Rediscover the difference by sampling organic carrots and butter, sourcing milk from heritage-breed cows and seeking out meat that has been raised and hung well. Rid your kitchen of products such as biscuits and flavoured crisps, shop-bought cakes and pies, margarine and low-fat foods, all of which have long lists of unwanted ingredients.

9
Ditch dieting

Change the way you think about food and you need never worry about dieting again. Eating mostly fresh, seasonal fare frees you from faddy diets and prevents the yo-yoing weight loss and gain that often accompanies dieting (and, dermatologists state, contributes to aged-looking skin). Instead of obsessing over the scales, judge your weight by how well your clothes fit.

10
Cut down on calories

If you are carrying excess weight and it won't budge, it may be because you now need fewer calories. Over 50s who aren't active need 200 fewer calories per day than those who lead a very physically active life. Adjust your diet to accommodate your slowing metabolism, for example by reducing portion size rather than by cutting out foods.

11
Appetite adaptations

As you age, you may find you can't tolerate large portions. Increase the amount of exercise you take to boost appetite: aim for 30 minutes a day. Make sure that what you do eat contains plenty of protein, vitamins and minerals, since these nutritional needs don't decline with the years.

12
Find more folate

Older people with low levels of folate have noticeably more memory problems than those whose diet is rich in this plant nutrient,

Colour and texture play an important role in healthy eating.

according to one study. To keep
mind and memory sharp, make sure
you eat some folate-rich, green leafy
vegetables and citrus fruit every day.

13

Choosing good carbs

Good carbohydrates are unrefined,
rich in nutrients and fibre, high
in flavour and keep you feeling
satisfied for hours. Aim for six
servings a day if you are not very
active; up to nine if you do more
exercise. Choose brown and wild
rices, oats, seeded wholemeal loaves,
wholewheat pasta. Even a home-
baked cake such as lemon cake
made with polenta and pistachios
supplies good carbs. If you're used
to fresh home-cooked food, bad
carbs are obvious because they
don't taste good: pappy white bread,
soggy processed quiche and pizza
bases, sugary breakfast cereals,
cake that never goes off. Avoid
them altogether.

14

Potato pleasures

Women who eat chips twice a week
increase their risk of contracting
type-2 diabetes, a major disease
affecting people post middle age,
according to one study. Opt instead
for organic potatoes baked, boiled
in their skins or mashed with
garlic and olive oil. Alternatively,
try flavourful sweet potatoes.

15

Eat whole grains

Fibre-rich whole grains are a
particularly good food choice as we
age. In one study, people over 60
who ate the most whole grains were
less likely to suffer metabolic
syndrome, a group of symptoms
implicated in heart disease and
diabetes. They were slimmer, too.
Whole grains are also rich in B
vitamins and magnesium. Brown
rice, for example, contains double
the magnesium of white rice.
A magnesium-rich diet is also
essential for bone density. Choose
organic to avoid pesticide residue.

16

Try ancient grains

Give unusual grains space in your
diet: try baking with spelt flour,
making salads using quinoa, and
planning breakfast around oats.
Many nutritionists feel these
overlooked grains are particularly
well adapted to the human
digestive system.

17

Source good bread

Home-baked bread warm from the
oven is a foodie's ultimate everyday
treat, dunked in a little pungent
olive or nut oil or spread with a little
good butter. Try to wean yourself
off supermarket bakeries and

Whole grains are so nutritious they
should be key to any anti-ageing diet.

additive-loaded sliced loaves. Search
for an artisan baker who sells bread
that goes hard after a day (a good
freshness test). Check out sour-
dough loaves, rye breads, mixes with
grains and seeds and Middle Eastern
flat breads. When you have time,
buy fresh once or twice a day, as is
traditional in France. Or bake your
own overnight in a bread machine.

18

Fat facts

Make sure your fat intake comes
mostly from oily fish, avocados,
walnuts and other nuts, extra-virgin
olive oil and flaxseed oil. Dietary fat
is essential with age, especially if
you have a small appetite or are
frail. It speeds absorption of fat-
soluble vitamins and carotenoids,
offers energy and essential fatty
acids, brings flavour, especially in
meat, and reduces inflammation
in diseases such as rheumatoid

arthritis. Monounsaturated fats boost the health of the arteries and heart by increasing "good" and reducing "bad" cholesterol. They also decrease risk of breast cancer, according to a Swedish study. "Trans" fats are oils that have been hydrogenated to extend shelf life. They have no nutritional benefits, increase risk of coronary heart disease, and have also been linked with cancer and skin disease. They are found only in processed foods, and aren't always labelled, so avoid them by avoiding processed foods.

19

Eat butter

Go to the refrigerator now and throw away low-fat spreads and margarine. They taste nasty and are packed with additives you should avoid. Substitute organic butter – look for local farmhouse butter, which has a distinct crumbly texture. Use only a scraping if you are worried about the health risks of saturated fat, or drizzle on extra-virgin olive oil instead.

20

Selecting good sugar

For baking and to scatter over bitter food and drinks choose dark sugars: brown sugar contains molasses, a good source of iron, and is so flavourful a little goes a long way when stirred into puddings, porridge and drinks. By adding the sugar yourself, you can monitor how much you are taking on board. Buy organic and fair-trade if desired. Honey is a sweetener and an antioxidant with fantastic health-giving properties, used in hospitals for wound healing. Studies suggest it may help prevent heart disease and offer anti-cavity protection for teeth.

21

Avoid artificial sweeteners

Many popular artificial sweeteners contain ingredients which may be harmful to your health. Check for aspartame (E951), which produces the toxin methanol, which the body can process only in small amounts, and has been associated with headaches and menstrual problems. Saccharin (E954) has been linked with bladder cancer. Acesulfame K (E950) has also been linked with cancer, while sorbitol (E420) and mannitol (E421) are associated with bloating.

22

Discovering hidden sugar

It's difficult to keep to the World Health Organization's recommended daily limit for sugar (no more than 10 per cent of your daily food intake) when it appears in so many forms in packaged, processed foods. If any of the following come near the top of an ingredients list or the product

Savour the smell and taste of fresh home-baked bread or source good bread from a local baker.

contains more than one in addition to sugar, leave that breakfast cereal, ketchup or diet food on the shelf:

- dextrose
- glucose
- corn syrup
- sucrose
- fructose
- HFCS (high fructose corn syrup)

23

Protein provision

Aim for two servings of protein a day, from meat and fish, pulses, nuts or dairy produce. In one osteoporosis study, people with the highest intake of protein maintained bone mineral density significantly better than those who ate less.

24

Fish for health

Oily fish such as salmon, sardines and mackerel are high in omega-3 fatty acids, which protect brain and eye health, protect the heart, can ease depression and guard against inflammation that can cause stiff, painful joints. Aim for at least two portions a week.

25

Which fish is best?

Opt for small fish lower down the food chain, such as sardines, herring and anchovies, as well as wild salmon. These contain 16 times fewer PCBs (polychlorinated biphenyls – cancer-causing neurological toxins that accumulate in the body) than farmed salmon according to a study by the Environmental Working Group. Larger carnivorous fish higher up the food chain have been found to contain high levels of environmental pollutants, including mercury, dioxins and PCBs.

26

Red meat for iron

Red meat is a particularly good source of iron, which older people tend to be deficient in. Serve meat with green leafy vegetables and a glass of fresh orange juice to maximize absorption.

27

Choose free range

Beef from herds that graze on pasture contains more healthy fats than meat from animals fed on dry, sometimes additive-laced feeds.

Oily fish, such as mackerel and sardines, are rich in omega-3 fatty acids, which have many health benefits.

Free-range beef also contains a good amount of antioxidant selenium. Organic farmers usually keep fewer animals per acre and so their animal husbandry tends to be better. Artificial hormones and other additives are banned. This leads to better-tasting meat. If you are concerned by the expense, opt for cheaper cuts for stewing and other forms of long cooking, or eat less. Try game, such as rabbit, pheasant and quail, which tend to be free range.

28

Find a good butcher

Look for a butcher who sources locally and chalks up which farmer (and even which field) the stock comes from. A good butcher often makes his own sausages or buys them in from artisan producers. He will be able to recommend particular cuts and offer meat that is in season, such as game and spring lamb, and tends not to offer pre-packed portions: vacuum-packed meat doesn't look or taste so good.

29

Eating poultry

Chicken is a good source of selenium, involved in DNA repair and cancer protection; niacin, which helps protect brain function as we age; and vitamin B_6 for energy and healthy heart and blood vessels.

Choose free-range chicken fed an organic diet. To seal in flavour and moisture leave the skin on while cooking.

30

Leave processed meat on the shelf

For colon health don't include a great deal of processed or cured meat in your diet, urges a Canadian study. This includes bacon, hot dogs and salami. Preservative nitrites in salami and "pressed ham" have been associated with increased risk of colon disease. In the same study, choosing fresh red meat or chicken breast seemed to lower the risk of disease by 39 per cent.

31

Veggie protein

In recent years many research studies have underscored the health benefits of plant-derived protein as we age. Include nuts, seeds and fibre-rich pulses, such as black beans, in your diet daily for protection against heart disease and stroke.

Shopping for food

How you shop determines how well you eat. If you buy locally from farmers' markets and pick-your-own farms, speciality butchers, bakers and fishmongers, bijou cheese shops and good delis, the produce that reaches your plate will be full of flavour as well as fresh and nutritious.

32

Organic farming

Food that is certified organic comes from farms run by people who are more likely to care about the health of our soil, water and air, the living conditions of livestock, and the flora and fauna around the farm. Produce of organic farming is less likely to have trace residues of pesticides, artificial fertilizers and antibiotics, and is guaranteed free from GM (genetically modified) material. Organic certifiers permit only a small range of artificial additives to be used in processed foods while more than 500 may be used in non-organic foods.

33

Nutrients boost

Organic farming seems to boost nutrient content. A recent UK study found 71 per cent more omega-3 fats (best for the heart) in organic than conventionally farmed milk. In another study, organic spinach was shown to have 100 per cent more iron and manganese than regular crops; deficiencies of both minerals are common in later life. The antioxidant vitamin E has been found to be as much as 50 per cent more potent in organic crops.

34
Organic priorities

Add a few organic staples to your shopping basket each week if you can't afford to convert to a totally organic diet. American magazine *Worth the Money* suggests prioritizing the following foods:

- dairy foods
- poultry and eggs
- meat
- apples and pears
- raspberries and strawberries
- cherries
- nectarines and peaches
- non-American grapes
- celery and peppers
- potatoes

35
Eating local

Faced with the choice between organic produce from the other side of the world and locally produced non-organic foods, go for the local option to reduce environmental pollutants resulting from transport

that may have an ageing effect on body systems. Local food should not have spent too long in storage and so may contain more vitamins.

36
Read the labels

Examine the ingredients listing of every item you pick off the shelf. If you don't understand any of the words or chemical formulae, replace the product and look for one with a shorter ingredients list, and one which you don't need a Masters degree to decipher.

37
Visit farmers' markets

With the best produce from miles around gathered in one place for a day, a farmers' market is as much a social occasion as a shopping opportunity. Enjoy meeting the

producers and quiz them about their use of pesticides, antibiotics and methods of animal husbandry. Ask how you tell whether produce is fresh, and enquire after cooking and juicing tips. Don't go with recipes in mind, rather pick up what looks best on the day and let that inspire the day's main meal.

38
Follow your senses

At the farmers' market, be tempted by your nose and eyes into trying something new every week – maybe an artisanal cheese, a type of fish or sausage you've never tasted, local flower honey or an old variety of apple. Ask stall-holders for preparation tips and to recommend good ingredient combinations.

39
Pick your own

In soft fruit season, head out to a pick-your-own farm to harvest strawberries, raspberries and other delicate fruit that doesn't travel well when ripe. Eat as many as you can fresh, then freeze or preserve the rest for a dose of cheering sunshine during dark winter months. This makes a great bonding family outing that appeals to children and grandchildren of all ages.

Get outdoors and pick your own fruit while it's still warm from the sun.

40

Source direct from the farm

Cut down on food miles and enjoy the destressing effect of knowing exactly where your food comes from by buying direct from a farm. Look for meat freezer packs and schemes that deliver to your doorstep.

41

Champion heritage varieties

Local breeds have lost out in past decades to livestock that is cheap to raise, but bland to the palate. Help revive taste history by joining the increasing numbers of chefs and shoppers returning to older, more unusual varieties, which are often more suited to regional climates and cuisines. Rare-breed meat is more likely to have been raised on family farms in free-range conditions with a varied diet, and to have been slaughtered humanely and properly hung. For all these reasons it tastes rich and well-textured, and offers a good balance between lean meat and flavour-enhancing fat.

42

Buy fair

Seek out fairly traded goods for a daily feel-good fix. Feeling uplifted by your ability to make a difference in the world every time you drink a cup of coffee or eat a banana is an

Food shopping is a destressing treat when stalls look this good.

easy stress-beater. People who retain a positive state of mind as they age live longer, happier lives.

43

Special occasions

When planning a meal to celebrate a birthday or anniversary why not turn to local producers to impress your guests? Put together hampers of cured meat, smoked fish, cheeses, fruit and loaves and head out to a nearby beauty spot.

44

Supermarket savvy

Get to know how supermarkets work so it's easier to resist the lure of unhealthy processed foods. Fresh produce – milk, fruit and vegetables, fish and meat counters – are usually sited around the perimeter of the store. Venture into the centre, where snack foods and ready meals lurk, for olive oil and wine only when you are ready to leave.

45

Take your own bag

Reduce the amount of plastics accumulating in the environment and the toxins created by their manufacture and disposal by taking cloth bags and wicker baskets on shopping trips instead of using plastic bags. Keep a fold-out string bag in your handbag for carrying any spontaneous lunch-hour purchases.

Healthy eating habits

How you eat helps turn back the clock. Missing breakfast, snacking on the run and grazing while watching TV are all associated with eating excess calories and foods low in vital nutrients. Most of all they preclude the joy of sharing food with people you love. Those who have a close network of family and friends to share mealtimes with tend to live longer more fulfilled lives.

Engaging the senses when eating allows you to appreciate and savour the food on your spoon.

46
Rituals of eating

Think of meals as sacrosanct times during the day when you stop and relax. Make sure you set aside enough time for food preparation, eating and clearing away. Eat sitting at the table to aid digestion and to allow you to savour the texture, colour and scent of food: enjoying food is as much to do with these sensations as with taste.

47
Laying the table

To give mealtimes a sense of occasion, clear from the table everything except food-related items. Put away work files, homework and unpaid bills. Throw over a clean tablecloth, place some fresh flowers or a candle in the centre, add a jug of water with ice and lemon, and lay cutlery, glassware and napkins. Choose co-ordinating plates and warm them before serving food.

48
Stop multi-tasking

Stop doing anything other than eating at mealtimes. Research suggests that people who eat while on the internet, working, driving or chatting on the phone tend to eat more than those who eat without distraction simply because they are not focused on the act of eating.

49
Ban TV dinners

The first rule of natural eating is to turn off the TV, because it diverts attention from the quality of your food and the quantity you are eating.

50
Put down your fork

Between mouthfuls put down your knife and fork. If your fingers feel restless, place them on your lap, palms facing upward. Enjoy the sensation of chewing and appreciate

the release of flavours. Chewing and savouring food not only aids digestion, it turns a meal from a period of processing, where speed is the focus, to a time of delight.

51
Count each chew

Chew each mouthful until every last vestige of taste has been given up and the food is small enough to swallow easily. Chewing triggers the release of enzymes and fluids that ensure easy and proper digestion.

52
Eating meditation

Don't miss out on the spirit-refuelling possibilities of eating with all your senses engaged. **Before sitting down to eat**, make sure you are hungry. Sit upright, close your eyes, and focus within.

Open your eyes and look at your plate, as if for the first time: examine the blend of colours and textures, steam rising or beads of oil. When other thoughts arise, let them pass; bring your awareness back to the food in front of you.

As you cut and spear, appreciate the textures: crisp, tender, oozing. Close your eyes, place a morsel in your mouth and feel the sensations as flavours activate tastebuds on various parts of your tongue.

After finishing, sit in silence briefly and concentrate on your digestion. Visualize food circulating through your body systems and being transformed into energy.

Sociable mealtimes keep relationships alive.

53
No more grazing

Nibbling mindlessly between meals (and finishing up leftovers) is a surefire way to take on board calories without enjoying the experience of eating. If you fancy a snack, dedicate time to it.

54
Write it down

If you're unsure how healthy your diet is, start a food journal. Every day write down exactly what you eat, and when. After a week, scrutinize your results and try to recognize patterns. Do you slip into bad habits mid afternoon or when you get home from work? Are your cupboards packed with processed foods because you go to the supermarket when you are hungry or accompanied by kids?

55
Sharing meals

Food is most pleasurable when shared. Aim to eat at least once a day with those who share your home, or with friends if you live alone. You might only be able to sit down together for breakfast, but insist on it, even if it only lasts a few minutes.

At mealtimes, problems can be discussed, opinions expressed, relationships worked on, jokes enjoyed. Once a week try to organize a more formal meal with more than one course and wine, where children are expected to stay at the table and converse.

56
Stock the store cupboard

Amass enough healthy staples to be able to throw together a healthy, tasty pasta dish in a hurry. Keep onion and garlic in the vegetable rack; extra-virgin olive oil, tinned plum tomatoes and tomato purée, anchovies and good spaghetti in the cupboard; black olives and parmesan cheese in the fridge.

57
Brush your teeth

Brushing teeth after meals has been shown in a Japanese study to be a habit associated with people who keep their weight at a healthy level.

58
Give thanks

Even if you don't say grace at mealtimes, think about all the people who made it possible for the food to reach your plate: farmers, transport workers, energy suppliers. Appreciate the interdependence of lives across the globe.

What to eat when

Listen to your body as well as your lifestyle when planning what to eat. Some of us do better on three meals a day, others prefer smaller portions more often. Make sure you have enough time between meals to relish the feeling of hunger that accompanies an empty stomach. Routine and regularity are the key to good nutritional health.

Oranges are a great source of potassium, folate, vitamin C and carotenoids.

59
Why breakfast matters

Kickstart the day with a good portion of the nutrients your body needs – without fuel body and mind won't cope with all your demands. Choose foods that offer a sustained energy boost: porridge, homemade muesli, wholemeal toast, eggs, yogurt with fruit, nuts and seeds.

60
Fresh orange juice

Squeeze it yourself and be sure that the fruit is organic, fairly traded, and not coated in petroleum waxes. Home-pressed orange juice with "bits" is a good source of potassium, folate, vitamin C, and carotenoids shown to reduce risk of an inflammatory condition that leads to rheumatoid arthritis by as much as 40 per cent.

61
Cardamom porridge

This recipe is inspired by a breakfast served at a food stall in the healing field at the Glastonbury festival. Serves four.

large mug organic jumbo porridge oats
2 mugs organic semi-skimmed milk
generous handful unsulphured
   dried apricots
8 cardamoms
maple syrup, to serve

Put the oats and milk in a large pan. Wash and finely chop the apricots and add. Bash the cardamoms to split them, then add to the pan. Slowly bring to the boil, stirring with a wooden spoon. Allow to bubble for a few minutes, then turn off and leave to cool for about 5 minutes, stirring occasionally. Serve with maple syrup.

62

Go to work on an egg

Eggs are always a good way to start the day for a high-quality protein hit, containing antioxidant selenium, choline for memory, and vitamin D, which helps calcium absorption and boosts immunity.

63

Keep chickens

The best eggs are freshly gathered from your own chickens. Even a small urban garden can be home to a couple of hens. If you don't want to construct your own coop and run, visit www.omlet.co.uk for its award-winning "eglu" – a small, pod-like coop, delivered complete with two organic laying hens, a fox-proof run, and the lure of 12 eggs per week.

64

Don't snack after exercise

A post-workout nutrition bar or glucose drink may seem tempting, but don't succumb if you want to keep trim. Go for green or camomile tea and an apple instead.

65

Spice up your life

Buy a book about Indian cuisine, grind your own curry powders and garam masalas, and aim to cook your own once a week. India has the lowest incidence of Alzheimer's disease in the world. Researchers attribute this to curry, which almost always contains turmeric, the main constituent of which, curcumin, seems to slow the progress of neurodegeneration. It is also a helpful anti-inflammatory for swollen joints and has been

66

Home-made muesli

Making your own muesli allows you to pander to personal preference. You can include anti-ageing seeds and nuts and leave out the ingredients you dislike.

- organic jumbo oats
- walnuts
- almonds
- Brazil and cashew nuts
- sunflower seeds
- pumpkin seeds
- pine nuts
- sesame seeds

1 Into a large bowl empty a bag of jumbo oats. Stir in as many of the nuts and seeds listed above as you wish. Pour the muesli into a large jar and seal tightly. Store in a cool dark place.

2 Each morning spoon out a bowlful of muesli. Add chopped fresh or soaked dry fruit to taste – kiwi for morning pep or traditional apple – then top up with semi-skimmed milk or yogurt.

associated with healthy cells. Other fabulously anti-ageing ingredients in the curry mix include ginger, garlic, chillies, fenugreek seeds, tomatoes and onions.

67
Adopt a Mediterranean diet

Benefit from this health-enhancing way of eating by building your daily diet around antioxidant-loaded fresh fruit and vegetables, highly nutritive whole grains and nuts, and heart-friendly olive oil and fish. In a recent study those who ate Mediterranean for just three months reduced their risk of cardiovascular disease by 15 per cent.

68
Eat with the seasons

Ayurveda, the Indian system of natural healthcare, is also referred to as the art of longevity. It teaches that body and mind become better balanced if we consume the produce of the seasons. Doing so aligns us with the rhythms of the natural world, echoing the earth's changes as the globe turns.

69
Spring clean

With the first buds of spring, make changes in your diet and introduce lighter foods that are easy to digest. Lighten up by easing back on dairy foods and rich, oily meals and gradually introduce more salads and bitter leaves, light broths, sprouted seeds and raw foods into your diet.

70
Summer foods

In the heat of summer, nature offers juicy fruit and water-laden vegetables to cool and hydrate the body, so take advantage of cucumber, courgettes, celery, watercress and flush-reducing watermelon. Major on chilled soups, cool juices and frozen yogurt. Make fresh mixed-leaf salads to keep active bones strong and calm the nerves with their sedative qualities.

71
Summer salad

Take large bunches of several leafy seasonal herbs, such as mint, parsley, coriander and sorrel. Wash, chop and dress with lemon juice, olive oil, salt and pepper. Slice feta cheese and stir in. Chill before serving.

Eating Mediterranean style is all about health-enhancing food and wine – and setting aside time to cook, prepare, eat and relax after eating.

The best mood-lifting treats are homemade from fresh ingredients.

72
Autumn foods

In the season of change, start eating more sweet, astringent and bitter-tasting foods, such as pumpkin, beetroot and parsnip, suggests Ayurveda. Keep the food light and easily digestible – it's not winter yet.

73
Root salad

Savour the earthy sweetness of carotenoid-rich carrots and red beetroot in a robust, clean-tasting cold-season salad. Serves four.

4 carrots
2 beetroot (uncooked)
generous handful sunflower seeds
balsamic vinegar, to taste

Grate the carrots and beetroot. Toast the sunflower seeds and toss into the salad while warm. Dress with a little balsamic vinegar.

74
Winter warmers

Ayurveda suggests we build in more sustaining, warming food in winter: go for hearty casseroles and roast joints, baked dishes based on dried legumes and root vegetables.

75
Vegetarian roast

Roast winter vegetables, such as carrot, parsnip, red beetroot and whole heads of garlic. Serve topped with grilled goat's cheese, or as wholemeal bread sandwiches.

76
Cheering treats

Don't be scared of the occasional treat: a mood-lifting glass of champagne with lunch, for example. Other treats include:

- 70 per cent cocoa, solid organic chocolate
- real ice cream from a dairy farm
- gourmet honey drizzled over toast or yogurt
- fine cheeses served with quince paste or ripe figs
- freshly made pancakes
- freshly popped corn
- homemade fruit scones served with good jam and clotted cream

77
Waist watching

Enjoying a treat early in the day seems to have less effect on the waistline. Alternatively, do more exercise to keep your waist in check.

78
Try fasting

In all the great religions, fasting is a tool of meditation, used as a way of reining in the excesses of body and mind. If you are in good health, you might like to have a juice and water-only day once every season. Alternatively, give up something you crave for a set period of time, and notice how after a while the cravings cease and your mind feels calmer.

Age-defying superfood

Research is showing us that some foods are particularly effective at keeping at bay the body's ageing mechanisms. Many of these superfoods are fruit and vegetables famed for their antioxidant powers – the more of these you can weave into your day, the better you protect body and brain from the ravages of time.

Blueberries may help safeguard memory.

79
Rewrite your shopping list
A recent report in the *British Medical Journal* suggested that eating certain key foods every day could boost cardiovascular health and even increase life expectancy by up to 6½ years. The items to keep a ready supply of are vegetables, fruit, garlic, almonds, wine, fish (twice a week) and dark chocolate.

80
Graze on grapes
Keep black grapes handy to pick at. The red colouring contains very potent antioxidants effective in maintaining youthful arteries. They are also a source of ellagic acid, associated with cancer-prevention.

81
Pomegranate power
The succulent seeds and juice of this fruit contain very high levels of antioxidant polyphenols that seem to protect against many diseases of ageing, including ailments of the heart and blood vessels. They also seem to inhibit the growth of prostate and breast cancer cells.

82
Cultivate peppers
Buy young pepper plants and nurture in pots through the summer ready to harvest in autumn. Like pumpkin and other red, orange and yellow fruit and vegetables, peppers contain the carotenoid beta-cryptoxanthin, which can help cut the risk of a precursor disease to rheumatoid arthritis by up to 40 per cent. Red peppers contain three times more vitamin C than citrus fruit.

83
Eat more berries
Eating dark red or purple berries boosts memory function. Blackcurrants and boysenberries are rich in the antioxidant flavonoid anthocyanins and seem to fight cell and DNA damage, which can contribute to the development of Alzheimer's and cancer. Blackcurrants, blackberries, bilberries and blueberries benefit ageing eyes and capillary walls, too. Eat fresh berries in season. Out of season try frozen or freeze-dried.

84
Enjoy nuts
Walnuts are renowned in Chinese medicine as the longevity fruit. As well as snacking on fresh shelled nuts, try using the oil in cooking and salad dressings. Packed with heart-protecting antioxidants and fats, walnut oil has a nutty flavour that works well with potatoes and other root vegetables. Peanuts share their cholesterol-lowering properties and are also linked to a decreased risk of heart disease. Eat a handful of almonds each day for their healthy monounsaturated fats, which are associated with a lowered risk of coronary heart disease and stroke.

85

Snack on seeds

Just a fistful of seeds a day is immensely protective, since they contain protein, useful amounts of minerals and fatty acids essential for joint and prostate health. Add pumpkin, flaxseeds (linseeds), sesame and sunflower seeds to muesli, scatter over salads and keep ready-mixed packets in your desk to dip into when energy levels drop.

86

Probiotic booster

A pot of organic live natural yogurt each day can help boost immunity. A Swedish study shows those who get a daily dose of the good bacteria, or probiotics, found in live or "bio" yogurt are less likely to call in sick than colleagues who don't. It's also good for digestive health and strong bones. If you find yogurt unpalatable, try drizzling over organic runny honey, adding chopped pistachio nuts or a spilling of fresh pomegranate seeds.

87

Eat fish twice a week

Dining on fish two to four times a week reduces the risk of heart disease by 14 per cent; eaten just once a week it can slow mental decline by 10 per cent a year in older people, studies suggest. As well as providing omega-3 fatty acids, oily fish offer antioxidant selenium, vitamin D, which seems to protect against forms of cancer common in older age, and magnesium, necessary for strong bones. The fatty acids in fish oils also counteract the effects on the heart of air pollutants, which increase risk of heart disease.

Olive oil has protective effects against many later-life illnesses.

88

Cook with garlic

Valuable for lowering blood pressure, reducing cholesterol, preventing blood clots and giving the immune system a powerful boost, eating 2 or 3 cloves of garlic daily can reduce by a quarter the risk of stroke and heart attack. Pound the cloves in a pestle and mortar or slice finely with a knife; in a garlic crusher cloves can take on a metallic tang. Use garlic fresh in salad dressings or add right at the end of cooking to ensure valuable compounds aren't destroyed by heat.

89

Switch to olive oil

You can substitute olive oil for other cooking oils, use it in salad dressings, drizzle it over crusty bread or use it as a massage and body oil. A diet rich in olive oil is associated with a 25 per cent reduced risk of coronary heart disease. Extra-virgin olive oil contains most anti-inflammatory and clot-preventing antioxidant phenols. Its main constituent, oleic acid, helps maintain healthy levels of cholesterol and seems to inhibit a gene that stimulates breast cancer cells. It's no wonder that the Mediterranean diet, with olive oil always on the menu, is associated with long life.

Laden with lycopene: aim for 10 servings of tomatoes a week.

baking, roasting or frying. The colour indicates the benefits: carotenoid pigment safeguards the skin and eyes as we age, and people with raised levels of beta-carotene show a reduced risk of developing rheumatoid arthritis. Vitamins C and E in the potatoes boost the carotenoids' antioxidant capabilities.

93
Broccoli for breasts

Boost breast health by eating one portion of steamed broccoli or other cruciferous greens, such as cabbage, kale and Brussels sprouts, most days. This seems to keep breast tissue healthy and helps rid the body of an oestrogen linked with the development of breast cancer. Broccoli is also high in bone-building calcium and folate, essential for artery health.

90
Keep ketchup on the table

Concentrated cooked tomato products, such as ketchup and purée, contain remarkably effective amounts of lycopene, the antioxidant red pigment found in red fruit and vegetables. In a large-scale European study, men with the highest intake of lycopene-rich foods were half as likely to suffer from a heart attack than those whose diets featured the lowest amount. Lycopene protects the heart and is good for blood pressure, suggests a recent study, and is also known to combat prostate cancer. The darker the fruit, the more lycopene it contains. Aim for a mighty 10 servings of fresh and cooked tomatoes a week, making sure they are organic: organic ketchup contains 83 per cent more lycopene than non-organic.

91
Salsa with everything

Capsaicin, the property that gives chillies heat, seems to kill liver and prostate cancer cells, studies suggest. Chilli peppers also protect against heart disease, high blood pressure, blood clots and high cholesterol. To make salsa, chop finely and stir together red onion, diced fresh tomatoes, coriander leaves, lime juice and enough of your favourite variety of chilli to achieve the heat level you prefer. Keep it in the fridge to accompany eggs at breakfast, omelettes at lunch and to pep up grilled meat or fish.

92
Substitute sweet potato

Once a week or more substitute orange-fleshed sweet potato for your regular carbohydrate: try

94
Eat your greens

The ageing brain stays sharper if you eat greens, according to a recent study. People who ate most folate-rich leafy greens and citrus fruit stayed significantly sharper and had better memories than those who ate fewer. Food sources might be more effective than taking a supplement. Other research shows that those who ate foods rich in folate reduced their risk of pancreatic cancer, whereas those who took a supplement didn't.

95

Garnish with herbs

Adding fresh herbs to dishes has been shown in research by the US Department of Agriculture to add more antioxidant properties to meals than the fruit, vegetable and berry ingredients. Maintain a constant supply of fresh basil, parsley and coriander by nurturing plants in pots in the kitchen. Plant a bay tree in a pot outside, and raise a rosemary bush and sage plants for marinades and stuffing roasts.

96

Citrus fruit salad

Slice and mix together oranges, strawberries and ripe mangoes (for vitamin C), peaches and fresh or dried apricots (for beta-carotene), and tangerines (for zeaxanthin), all essential for eye health as we age. Drizzle over orange juice and spike with Cointreau for special occasions. Age-related macular degeneration is a prime cause of blindness in the over 55s, and people with a higher intake of these nutrients are significantly less likely to develop the condition.

97

Serve organic milk

Calcium for bone health seems to be best absorbed from dairy products. Select organic milk because, according to EU studies, it contains 70 per cent more omega-3 fatty acids and higher levels of vitamins A and E than non-organic milk. It also has 75 per cent more beta-carotene and two to three times higher levels of the antioxidant plant chemicals lutein and zeaxanthin. Buy milk in a carton rather than a bottle because nutrients are lost on exposure to light. Older women should drink four glasses of low-fat organic milk a day to help guard against osteoporosis. If you find this quantity a tall order, supplement with yogurt and cheese.

98

Daily chocolate

It's healthy to enjoy fine chocolate in moderation thanks to the amazingly antioxidant polyphenols it contains. Eating chocolate daily can reduce risk of circulation problems by 27 per cent, lower blood pressure, increase "good" cholesterol and inhibit blood clotting, suggest studies. Choose dark chocolate rich in cocoa solids (look for 70 per cent or over) and stick to moderate amounts. Try making your own chocolate drinks with fairly traded cocoa and just enough dark sugar to sweeten to taste. Milk chocolate bars containing sugars and hydrogenated oils don't share the benefits.

Indulge and enjoy: fine, dark chocolate is rich in antioxidants.

Food away from home

Dining and snacking away from home need not be a nutritional nightmare if you follow a few simple rules and keep a good stock of healthy, anti-ageing foods in your handbag or on your desk at work.

99
Mid-morning hunger
If you need a pick-me-up to tide you over until lunchtime, reach for a banana, a few dried prunes or a handful of nuts and seeds to stabilize energy highs and lows.
- Brazil nuts will boost your levels of antioxidant selenium.
- Walnuts are a good source of oil to ease inflammation.
- Pistachio nuts are rich in cholesterol-clobbering phytosterols.
- Sunflower seeds and cashew nuts help keep blood pressure healthy.
- Organic carrots: their pigment may reduce the risk of arthritis.
- Dried cranberries are a source of antioxidant vitamins A, C and E.

100
Beating the pm slump
If your eyes start to close mid-afternoon, go and breathe in some fresh air – without stoppping at the vending machine en route. When you get back to your desk, drink a reviving cup of peppermint tea and snack on one of the energy boosters listed in No. 99.

101
Emergency rations
Carry the following in your bag for times when hunger or thirst strike on the run: sachets of green tea, a bottle of mineral water, an apple, small pack of raisins, easy-peel satsuma and oat cakes.

102
Carry an apple
The ultimate portable health food, apples really do keep the doctor away, suggest researchers at Cornell University, because they contain some of the highest levels of the flavonoid quercetin, a potent antioxidant plant pigment. Red apples provide the most. Flavonoid-rich foods also have antiviral, antibacterial and anti-inflammatory effects, and seem to protect against heart disease, stroke, bowel cancer and Alzheimer's disease. Make sure you eat the skin, where flavonols concentrate.

103
Street food
Street food provides some of the freshest, best-tasting snacks: doughnuts fried while you wait then dunked in sugar, fish and chips by the seashore, cartons of stir-fried noodles direct from the wok at street markets. Enjoy such high-fat snacks occasionally for the youth-inducing joy of eating for pleasure.

104
Dining out without pigging out
When eating in restaurants, start with a glass of water and salad. Those who eat greens at the beginning of a meal tend to eat fewer calories in total, according to one study. To prevent the feeling of an uncomfortably full stomach, stay away from side dishes and order a main course that entails a lot of handling for small results: a platter

In restaurants opt for time-consuming, fiddly food such as shellfish platters.

of seasonal local seafood is a good source of antioxidant selenium and the tiny portions call for effort of fingers and brain, as does plucking leaves from a globe artichoke to dip in vinaigrette. If you fancy something sweet to finish, but don't want to suffer energy dips later, share a pudding.

105
Eating outdoors

Food always tastes better outdoors, especially when you have had to work for it by building a fire or walking to a spectacular spot. In the summer, plan picnics, beach barbecues, clam bakes or garden parties. In winter, throw potatoes and bananas into the embers of a bonfire.

106
Perfect picnic kit

Having the right kit makes every picnic more of an occasion, and food tastes better outdoors from real china and glass. Keep the following ready for impromptu outings:
- wicker picnic basket
- corkscrew and Swiss army knife
- cushions for lounging
- real glasses and cutlery
- china or enamel plates
- linen napkins
- gingham tablecloth
- plaid picnic blanket
- ice pack for cooling wine

Eating from scratch

When you cook meals from fresh, you can be sure you are preserving all the natural ingredients. Rather than seeing cooking as a chore, regard it as part of a healthy lifestyle, keeping you in touch with the seasons and allowing you to switch off from work and family issues.

107
Quality ingredients

When you choose quality ingredients, preparing food is simple. Leave produce in as fresh a state as you can to enjoy flavours and textures the way nature intended. Eating fruit and vegetables raw and tossed in salads means no vitamins or anti-ageing plant nutrients are lost in heating.

108
Conserve taste and nutrients

Preserve as much folate and vitamin C as possible in vegetables by steaming rather than boiling. This helps maintain flavour, too. Stir-frying is also good for conserving taste and nutrients.

109
Deli entertaining

Informal entertaining is easy with good deli produce. Offer a platter of locally produced cheeses and cold meats, served with fresh crusty bread and an interesting salad or two or a fresh soup. Buy dessert from a patisserie, try organic farm ice cream or provide a bowl of ripe seasonal fruit.

110
Pack your lunch box

Ditch the sandwich counter and start making up your own lunch box. It might include:
- cottage cheese with walnuts and chopped dried apricots
- homemade humus with crudités: broccoli florets, slices of red pepper and carrots, celery sticks, cucumber and cherry tomatoes
- kale coleslaw, with grated apple and carrot
- open sandwiches on dark rye bread
- avocado: slice in half, add a splash of balsamic vinegar
- iron-rich watercress soup made with a little onion and potato
- tabbouleh, soaked bulgar wheat with olive oil and lemon juice, chopped mint and parsley

111

Instant good food

Shift your daily menus to fresh instant food rather than microwaved ready meals. Grill asparagus spears for a few minutes on each side and finish with a squeeze of lemon, a little olive oil and some shavings of parmesan cheese. Asparagus is a good source of folate, essential for memory retention. Other ideas for meals in minutes include:

- omelettes
- poached salmon
- grilled sardines
- steak sandwich
- smoked mackerel
- stir-fried noodles and mixed vegetables
- whole fresh sweetcorn, boiled and buttered

112

Effortless meals

Slow cooking can be effortless, too. Throw potatoes in a slow oven a couple of hours ahead of supper time. Serve with cold chicken or cheese and salads. Roast slices of squash and sweet potato, carrots, onions and whole garlic cloves. Stir into couscous fluffed up with olive oil and butter to help your body absorb the antioxidant nutrients.

113

Slow soups

Roughly chop leeks, onions, celery and potatoes. Sweat in a little olive oil, then pour over stock, cover and allow to simmer until soft. Repeat the formula with other combinations of vegetables, try broths, minestrones and miso soup, make lentil-based dhals or throw in

114

Making aïoli

This garlic mayonnaise recipe is more than delicious, it is an exercise in slow cooking – and every ingredient is anti-ageing. Make sure the egg is super fresh.

- 2 cloves garlic, to taste
- large pinch sea salt
- free-range organic egg, separated
- approximately 200ml extra-virgin olive oil
- organic lemon, halved

1 Using a large pestle and mortar, pound the garlic with the salt until a soft purée is formed. Mix the egg yolk into the purée.

2 Drop by drop add the oil, stirring constantly with a wooden spoon, always in the same direction. Don't let your mind wander.

3 Keep stirring in oil until the mixture stands up in firm peaks – you may not need it all. Stir in a squeeze of lemon juice and chill.

some black beans or other fibre-rich legumes to reduce risk of heart disease and stroke. Research shows that supping soup makes us feel full and so stops snacking. Soup-eaters lose weight more easily than those who eat the same calories in other forms.

115
Keep something healthy in the fridge

Make up simple soups and pasta sauces in advance. Refrigerate so they can be heated up in minutes when you get in from the office or the gym.

116
Sprouting seeds

Sprouted seeds are living foods. Buy a sprouter and harvest mung beans, alfalfa, mustard and cress for an easy-to-digest energy boost. They are packed with protein, enzymes, minerals and antioxidant vitamins.

117
Free your mind

Instead of slavishly following recipes, close the book after you have cooked a dish a couple of times and experiment – focus on flavours, varying vegetables and herbs to adapt the dish to suit the changing seasons and personalities of guests. Using your brain keeps it active.

118
Tasty leftovers

Roast an organic chicken or joint of free-range lamb or beef. Enjoy hot. Eat cold with fresh vegetables, salsas and salads next day for an instant healthy meal.

119
Colourful stir-fries

Stir together finely sliced colourful vegetables: carrots, red onions, red, orange and yellow peppers, broccoli and kale. Throw in a handful of

Stir-frying keeps food colourful and full of flavour and nutrients.

sliced almonds and some mangetout. Experiment by adding beansprouts, noodles, seaweed, seafood or tofu.

120
Quick pasta sauce

Toss artichoke hearts and shelled peas in olive oil to warm through then stir into cooked pasta, adding torn fresh basil or mint to garnish. Peas are the richest source of vitamin B_1 and fresh peas have been shown to enhance sleep, raise a jaded appetite and boost cheerfulness.

121
Summer salads

Make up exciting combinations featuring watercress, barely cooked broccoli, sliced red pepper and ripe tomatoes, avocado, courgette slices brushed with olive oil and grilled,

Growing cress allows you to eat fresh home-grown greens throughout the year – even in the depths of winter.

grilled goat's cheese and toasted pine nuts. Dress with olive oil and balsamic vinegar.

122
Youthful salad dressing

Make up in advance and refrigerate to use throughout the week. Cider vinegar is regarded as the essence of youth in some parts of the world.

1 tbsp cider vinegar
1 tbsp flaxseed or hemp oil
5–6 tbsp extra-virgin olive oil
1 tsp Dijon mustard
1–2 tsp runny organic honey
pinch herbes de Provence
sea salt and freshly ground
   black pepper

Place the vinegar in a lidded jar. With a fork, whisk in the flaxseed or hemp oil until amalgamated. Add the olive oil until the taste suits you. Add the mustard, honey and herbs, and whisk again until smooth. Season to taste. Lid and refrigerate. Shake before serving.

123
Homemade freezer foods

This is the answer to effortless healthy home-cooked food when you are too tired to lift a finger. When you do have time, perhaps at a weekend, make up double quantities or more, then freeze your own ready meals. In summer, freeze whole berries to use in winter smoothies, pies and desserts.

Drinking water

One of the best – and cheapest – anti-ageing tonics is to drink plenty of water. Hydration from within makes your skin look less tired, helps fend off headaches, digestive problems and tiredness and reduces food cravings. It also boosts concentration, energy levels and nutrient delivery as well as flushing toxins from the system.

124
Water cure

The sensation of thirst declines with age. Make sure you don't become dehydrated by drinking six to eight glasses of water (about 2 litres/ 3½ pints) daily, especially in summer and when working in air-conditioned or centrally heated rooms.

125
Store in glass

If you buy mineral water choose brands in glass bottles because plastic (especially polycarbonate, with the recycling triangle mark 7) taints the taste of water and may leach the hormone-disrupting chemical bisphenol-A. Store tap water in the fridge in glass jugs or stainless steel.

126
Still or sparkling?

Carbonated water has had a bad press but a study of Spanish women found it had no effect on bone density. Another study carried out on American cyclists showed that fizzy water has no adverse effects on the digestive system.

127
Drink enough water

Drink a glass of water on getting up and make another glass the last liquid you sip before bed. When you work, drink often from a glass of water close to your desk and take regular water-cooler breaks to fill up. Keep a bottle of water by your side at the gym.

Body and brain need constant rehydration to help them function at optimum levels.

128
Fizzy drinks make you fat
Opt for plain or sparkling water over carbonated sugary drinks. A recent US study showed drinking just one can a day can add 1 stone (7kg) to a person's weight over a year.

129
Citron pressé
Squeeze the juice of half an organic lemon into a glass. Top up with warm or sparkling water and sip for a morning pick-me-up that encourages digestion.

130
Find out about fluoride
High intake of fluoride may result in bones that become more brittle. Find out from your supplier if your water supply contains fluoride. If it does, you might like to avoid fluoride toothpaste.

131
Water filters
Use a water filter if it makes water more palatable. Filters that fit into a jug or kettle screen out heavy metals, such as lead and copper, but might not be effective against some pesticides and nitrates. A reverse-osmosis filter fitted beneath the sink is the only way to rid water of fluoride and many pesticides.

Organic juicing

Juicing fruit and vegetables makes available all the benefits of raw food without time-consuming chewing. If you juice at home you can be creative with combinations and be sure of the provenance of ingredients. Make the most of bags of organic juicing fruit sold cheaply at farmers' markets. If you find eating breakfast onerous, whizz up stoned, peeled fruit with yogurt, seeds and nuts for an easy-to-sip smoothie.

132
Flush-calming drinks
Mix pomegranate juice with freshly squeezed lime juice to cool the body. Alternatively, whizz up a spicy lassi. Blend yogurt with half the amount again of water. Stir in sugar or salt to taste, plus ¼ tsp each of crushed cardamom seeds and ground cinnamon.

Juicing fruit and vegetables brings the maximum nutritional benefit.

133
Perk-up juices
Juice combinations of fruits and vegetables make the most of their active ingredients:
- Red grapefruit juice reduces "bad" cholesterol (avoid if on medication).
- Tomato juice with a shake of celery salt, black pepper and Worcestershire sauce is a great morning pick-me-up.
- Carrot, apple and ginger combine for a spring detox.
- Celery, beetroot, spinach and apple with a squeeze of lemon juice are refreshing in the afternoon.
- Blackberries with fresh orange juice make a tart start to the day.

134
Heritage juices
For best flavour, look for cloudy speciality apple and pear juices from family orchards that specialize in named local varieties, each with a distinct taste.

135
Breakfast smoothies

Berry smoothie: blend 1 punnet of berries with 2–3 tbsp natural yogurt and top up with cold milk. Garnish with toasted nuts and seeds.

Banana-mango breakfast: whizz up the flesh of 1 banana and 1 mango; mix in yogurt to taste and 1 tsp each sesame seeds and flaxseeds (linseeds).

Tonic brews

Some herbal teas are instantly uplifting and calming against the ageing effects of stress and mental overload. Green tea is immune-strengthening and a fine antioxidant as well as good for the heart. Black tea and coffee, once considered a health no-no because of their caffeine content, are now regarded as tonic brews.

Green tea is a potent antioxidant and helps keep the mind sharp.

136
Drink a cuppa

Researchers from Tokyo Medical University have established that drinking black tea after high-fat meals helps blood circulation. Other research suggests people who drink four or more cups a day halve their risk of heart attack and also reduce high blood pressure. Drinking double this amount has been linked to a reduction in cancer risk.

137
Go green

A potent antioxidant, green tea has been found in studies to boost longevity and the immune system, cut risk of heart disease and reduce inflammation. Antibacterial and antiviral, it also helps stimulate the burning of calories according to researchers at the University of Geneva. Drinking more than two cups a day keeps mind and memory sharp with age. Japanese women who drink green tea also have lower risk of breast cancer and better outcomes if they do contract the disease. Aim for three to six cups a day.

138
Curry and green tea

When eating Indian-style curries, take a cup of green tea. Turmeric, a staple ingredient in Indian curries, and green tea seem to enhance each other's health-giving properties.

139
Try white tea

Although it originates from the same plant as green and black tea, *Camellia sinensis*, white tea contains more active ingredients, and so potentially more health benefits. Of all tea varieties, white tea is the least processed, which may be the source of its health-giving properties. The young buds are simply steamed and dried after picking, preserving the mix of antioxidant polyphenols. In China it is valued as meditation-enhancing, so drink before yoga.

140
Spiced tea

Brew tea the Indian way, as chai, to energize and aid digestion. Serves two.

3 cups of water
¼ tsp each crushed cardamom pods, ground cinnamon, freshly ground black pepper, ground ginger
3 tsp black tea leaves
semi-skimmed milk, to taste

In a pan bring the water to the boil with the spices. Add the tea and a generous slug of milk, if desired, and bring to the boil again. Steep for 5 minutes, then strain into cups. Chai is traditionally drunk sweetened.

141
Herbal teas to revive

• Peppermint tea is advised for instant brain recovery and to relieve stomach discomfort.

• Nettle tea helps maintain strong bones and is an antioxidant.

• Lemon balm tea refreshes in summer heat and stimulates brain and memory.

• Ginger tea gives instant zing and keeps joints mobile and circulation moving. Grate 2.5cm (1in) fresh ginger into a cup, pour over boiling water and steep for 10 minutes; sweeten with honey.

142

Herbal teas to calm

• Camomile tea is a natural sedative that brings relief for the digestion and stress headaches.

• Fennel tea is soothing for the digestive system.

• Elderflower tea calms symptoms in the hay-fever season.

143

Go for good coffee

Caffeine has given coffee a bad name, but research at Harvard Medical School suggests that drinking coffee in moderation lowers risk of type 2 diabetes. It also seems to enhance brain function, reduce risk of Parkinson's and may protect against colon cancer. However, more than three cups a day is associated in older women with loss of bone density. Aim to enjoy one really good cup of well-brewed fresh coffee rather than several cups of mediocre instant.

144

Don't take out toxins

When buying coffee to take away, avoid coffee shops that serve hot drinks in polystyrene cups, which might allow seepage of the toxins benzene and styrene into food.

145

Demand cocoa

Act elderly and demand to be served cocoa in bed. A cup of cocoa made with hot water contains twice as many protective antioxidant polyphenols as a glass of red wine; three times as many as a cup of green tea; and five times as many as black tea, suggests a study from Cornell University. There are concurrent benefits for heart health, circulation and glucose metabolizing. A Dutch study suggests older men who drink cocoa have lower blood pressure and may live longer than those who don't. Drink in moderation, making with cocoa powder and a little sugar to taste, rather than using hot chocolate mixes, which can be high in additives and trans-fatty acids implicated in risk of heart disease. The benefits of drinking cocoa made with hot milk have not been assessed.

Choose good coffee and drink in moderation with a little dark chocolate.

Age-defying alcohol

A little alcohol, especially red wine, seems to play an important role in keeping the body and brain feeling and acting youthful. Drinking one or two small glasses a day is associated with substantially lowered risk of coronary heart disease and Alzheimer's, as well as boosting immunity and reducing risk of stroke.

146
Tips for the party season

For times of the year when you simply must over-indulge, try these:

- Eat before a night on the town.
- Match each alcoholic drink with a glass of water.
- Stick to one type of drink.
- Beware of cocktails and alcopops: fruit flavouring and sweetness disguise alcoholic content.
- Don't allow your glass to be refilled until it's empty.

147
Avoid bingeing

Reserving the recommended number of units of alcohol for one weekly or monthly drinking session wipes out the benefits of a daily glass of wine. When bingeing becomes regular, it makes more likely some ailments associated with ageing, from cardiovascular disease, stroke and liver or kidney damage to breast cancer and osteoporosis.

148
Red wine benefits

Drinking a glass of red wine a day seems to have remarkable health effects, protecting the ageing heart and even guarding against gum disease, suggests a recent study, thanks to the presence of impressive amounts of antioxidant phenols which thin the blood and keep artery walls clear. Spanish studies

Enjoying one alcoholic drink every day is most heart-friendly.

found people who enjoyed two or more glasses a day suffered 44 per cent fewer colds than those who did not indulge.

149
Red or white?

Although white wine has health benefits, red wine seems to be more useful in the anti-ageing armoury. If you are trying to keep your weight down, be aware that a standard glass of sweet white wine contains almost 120 calories, compared to, on average, 85 in a glass of red wine.

150
Try organic wine

Sample organic wines for their lower levels of sulphites. Many people who drink organic wine report fewer allergic reactions and a less buzzy hangover. Look for Demeter-labelled biodynamic wines.

151
Beer benefits

A daily glass of beer reduces risk of contracting heart disease and cataracts by 50 per cent according to a Canadian study, since beer, like red wine, contains antioxidant phenols. Choose dark beers, such as ale or Guinness, which contain almost double the antioxidants of lager, or you might like to try German hemp beer.

152

Don't overdo it

Be aware that imbibing more than two glasses of wine every day of the week may make the complexion look older. An overtaxed liver can't function well enough to maintain healthy-looking skin tone and texture. Also, heavy drinking increases production of damaging free radicals while depleting antioxidant vitamins essential to skin health.

153

Alcohol-free days

Build non-drinking days into your week: two or three alcohol-free days give the liver time to recover. Anticipation can make a glass of wine taste all the more delicious.

154

Drink with meals

For optimum effects drink alcohol like the Mediterraneans, sipping a glass or two of wine with a meal. Drinking after your evening meal, especially after 10pm, when alcohol is metabolized less quickly, may interfere with clear thinking and the ability to make judgements, and can make deep sleep more elusive, being associated with night waking. Interrupted sleep is visible on the face as well as in lowered energy levels and memory skills.

Sipping a social drink with a meal benefits mental health as well as increasing longevity.

155

Make your own fruit punch

Apples, the basis of this warming festive punch, are valuable anti-ageing agents. Make the recipe using organic farmhouse cider for reduced amounts of sulphur dioxide and no artificial sweeteners. Makes enough for six glasses.

1 litre (2 pints) cider
8 cloves
5cm (2in) piece fresh ginger, peeled and finely chopped
4 russet apples, cored and sliced
2 unwaxed oranges, sliced

Place the cider in a large pan with the cloves, chopped ginger, apple and orange slices. Bring to a simmer (but do not allow to boil). Ladle into heatproof glasses.

156

Post-holiday liver detox

After a period of over-indulgence, take a two-week alcohol break, drinking nettle tea to support the kidneys and liver and for a mineral boost. Try a supplement of milk thistle – the active ingredient silymarin not only helps the liver clear alcohol from the body, it is also rich in antioxidants. Consult a herbalist or take 80–200mg, 1–3 times daily. (Consult your doctor if you are on medication, pregnant or using oral contraception.)

Beating cravings

No matter how good the intentions, it can be difficult to overpower cravings for junk food and unhealthy drinks. Some of these natural approaches may help. When you do give in, forgive yourself: if you are eating a diet based around fruit and vegetables and drinking lots of water, the occasional lapse is no cause for concern.

157
Keep a food diary

If some foods you crave don't leave you feeling too good, you may have an intolerance to them. Before visiting a doctor or nutritionist, keep a record of everything you eat or drink and your reactions to them for at least three days. Some foods are well known for causing reactions, so pay attention if symptoms such as bloating, headaches, fatigue or mood swings occur when you eat or drink dairy foods, wheat, citrus fruit, tomatoes, eggs, sugar or caffeine.

158
Changing habits

To banish something from your diet, ban it from the house. You can't eat what isn't there. Enlist your family in your campaign to cut back on biscuits or crisps by removing those foods from family meals and snack times. Go to the supermarket without the kids to avoid pester power. If it helps to take things slowly, banish problem foods from your home, but not entirely from your life – yet – by eating them only at friends' homes or in restaurants.

159
Switch chocolate treats

If chocolate is your destressing treat, switch from milk chocolate to cocoa-rich dark versions (look for those with 70 per cent or more cocoa solids). You'll find you need to eat less to feel the positive effects.

160
Enlisting help

Urge friends to text you uplifting messages randomly during the day. Your phone might just buzz as you are opening the fridge. Ask girlfriends to turn up not with a tempting cake, but with some exotic fruit or flowers instead. If they don't take the hint, invent a convenient allergy – wheat bloats you, sugar brings you out in hives…

161
Shop sated

Visit the supermarket on a full stomach, and take a list – both strategies help counter impulse-buying and stop you reaching for less healthy options with eye appeal, such as greasy pastries and fat-laden savoury snacks. Shopping online from a saved list also helps you hold out against bad impulse buys.

162
Herbal help

Herbalists recommend taking the herb kudzu to help eliminate cravings. In one study it seemed to repress the urge to binge drink. Ingredients in the herb are known to lower blood pressure, and may also increase blood flow to the brain. Kudzu contains oestrogen-like isoflavones, which may be helpful in the menopause. Consult a herbalist, a practitioner of Traditional Chinese Medicine or take 30–120mg two or three times a day.

163
Feel-good alternative

Try a quick breathing exercise when willpower wanes. Close your eyes and cut out thoughts and external pressure by noticing your breath move in and out. When your breathing pattern feels calmer, imagine exhaling toxins and negative thoughts with every out-breath. On each in-breath imagine your body being energized by cleansing oxygen that brings with it a new lease of life.

164
Aromatherapy fix

Place 2 drops of essential oil of grapefruit on a handkerchief. Inhale when you need a deterrent at the sweet counter. The Institute of Aromatherapy in Toronto suggests this curbs cravings for sweet treats.

165
Set short-term goals

Take things one day at a time, focusing on getting through the next 24 hours (or if this seems overwhelming, then opt for the next hour) without succumbing to food temptations. Whenever worries about tomorrow or next month come to mind, bat them away and return to thinking about today.

166
Treats matter

Reward yourself with a small treat for sticking to a healthy diet, such as a new lipstick or book, a plant for the garden or extra minutes in bed. To keep momentum going, build up to a big pat on the back, maybe a shoe-shopping session, or a visit to a day spa.

167
Avoid temptation

Remove easy temptation from your daily routine. Change your route to work if you can't pass the corner shop without buying crisps. If you usually binge on cocktails at a girlfriend's house, invite her out to a movie instead.

168
Healthy pick-me-ups

Try one or more of the following, which not only taste great and are something of a foodie treat, but also contain valuable amounts of nutrients and health-enriching plant substances: a handful of collagen-rich cherries; heritage varieties of apple (some taste like champagne); fresh or dried figs which are loaded with minerals including calcium; antioxidant red guava.

169
Visualization

When reaching for a snack bar, imagine your arteries furring up, your skin becoming more sallow and fleshy, your brain finding it harder to make connections. Then picture a shower of tropical rain pounding on your scalp, washing away these pictures. Sense a feeling of vibrancy and cleanliness inside and out.

170
Affirmations

Repeating motivational phrases helps reset your default. Persevere even if it makes you feel silly. Find a phrase that instils self-confidence and a sense of purpose, such as, "I am in control" or "I love food that's good for me". Repeat your phrase on waking and go to sleep with it echoing in your head.

Choose healthy treats, such as collagen-rich cherries, to brighten up your day.

When to supplement

Many people choose to fight the war against ageing free radicals by eating foods containing antioxidants, and by taking supplements, which contain larger doses of nutrients and plant compounds than are available from a regular diet. Consult a nutritional therapist to find out which supplements might suit you. If you are pregnant or taking medication, consult your doctor before using any.

171

Supplements vs food sources

Eat a variety of vitamin-rich foods rather than relying totally on vitamin and mineral supplements for cancer protection, suggests the US Department of Health. In some studies, patients taking supplements don't see the health benefits of those ingesting the same nutrients through food. This may be because of the synergistic reactions that take place when plant ingredients combine, setting up healing processes not yet understood by science.

172

Beware very high doses

Be wary of taking higher doses of antioxidants than recommended. In some cases they can act as pro-oxidants, which can damage the body. One advantage of getting nutrients directly from food sources is that it's almost impossible to overdose on them.

173

Support the heart

Co-enzyme Q_{10} keeps all parts of the body working well, and is essential for generating energy and for muscle function and stamina, but it declines in the body and is less easily absorbed after our 20s. An antioxidant, it may help treat heart disease and lower high blood pressure, and seems to have an anti-cancer action. It is also prescribed to prevent age-related memory loss and boost immunity. Food sources include sardines, peanuts and spinach, or take 50mg daily with food (consult your doctor if taking heart or blood-pressure medication).

174

Improve brainpower

The herb *Ginkgo biloba* has antioxidant properties and by promoting the tone and elasticity of blood vessels boosts circulation to the body's peripheries, including the brain. This has been linked in studies with modest improvements in memory in people with Alzheimer's, and with easing depression and anxiety in older people. Take 120mg daily (consult

Ginkgo biloba boosts blood circulation to the brain, improving brain power.

your doctor if taking blood-thinning or blood-pressure medication, insulin or antidepressants).

175
Keep joints mobile

The source of the healing power of evening primrose oil is its constituent omega-6 essential fatty acid GLA (gamma-linoleic acid), which the body converts into inflammation-controlling prostaglandins. The body converts dietary fat into GLA less efficiently as we age, making supplements popular. Taking evening primrose oil can lessen joint pain and swelling in rheumatoid arthritis, has the added advantage of keeping skin, hair and nails looking youthful and may be useful in keeping memory strong by boosting the transmission of nerve impulses. Take 1,000mg with food up to three times a day.

176
Build bones

Vital for energy production, metabolism, digestion and bone health, calcium-rich food and supplements reduce risk of bone loss and fracture, lower blood pressure, and keep the heart and blood vessels healthy. Calcium also protects against colon cancer, insomnia and migraines. Food sources include dairy foods, oily fish (eat the bones), eggs, nuts, sunflower and sesame

Evening primrose oil is great for hair, skin, nails, memory and keeps joints healthy.

seeds, dried figs and green leafy vegetables. Organic food has more calcium. Soak up the sun for 15 minutes daily to generate vitamin D, which is essential for calcium uptake, as is magnesium, available from nuts, whole grains and yeast extract. To ensure your intake is high enough take 1,000mg calcium a day to age 50, 1,200mg if you are over 50.

177
Boost energy

The amino acid L-carnitine, which helps the body make energy, is not available in large amounts in food, although it is found in meat, dairy produce and spinach. Studies suggest that taking 250–1,000mg daily can boost energy and endurance levels, help with age-related memory loss and also support the heart.

178
Universal antioxidant

Nutritionists may recommend taking L-carnitine with alpha-lipoic acid (ALA), the "universal antioxidant" that boosts energy production in body cells, relieves fatigue and increases the effectiveness of vitamins C and E. ALA seems to support healthy nerve, heart and liver function, and may improve long-term memory and prevent cataracts. It can be found in meat, yeast extract and spinach, but not in quantity. Take 100mg once or twice a day.

179
Protect the eyes

Antioxidant carotenoid pigments lutein and zeaxanthin act as nature's sunglasses, protecting eyes from sun damage and supporting the macula, part of the retina that degenerates with age, causing gradual loss of sight. High levels of lutein and zeaxanthin seem also to boost immunity and protect against heart disease, breast and lung cancer and age-related brain deterioration. Natural food sources are red peppers, pumpkin, carrots, sweet potatoes and sweetcorn; dark green vegetables such as spinach, broccoli and kale. Absorption from enriched eggs may be 200–300 per cent more efficient than from other food and supplements. Alternatively, take 6mg lutein and 0.1-0.2mg zeaxanthin daily.

180

Oil the heart

Most of us don't get enough omega-3 fatty acids from food. These essential fats underpin the healthy working of many body systems. They maintain low cholesterol and reduce blood pressure protecting the heart from disease, and thin the blood reducing risk of stroke. They also decrease inflammation and joint stiffness, and seem effective for mood disorders and depression. Omega-3 fats may have anti-cancer powers, too. Good food sources include mackerel, tuna, salmon, herring; venison and buffalo meat; flaxseeds (linseeds), walnuts and hemp oil. If you are worried about contamination of fish or you think

your intake is too low take a 2g supplement daily (consult your doctor if taking blood-thinning medication).

181

Fight disease

Selenium is a trace element required by every body cell. It is vital in disease prevention because it helps antioxidant enzymes to function. Selenium also protects against heart attack and stroke, cataracts and macular degeneration. Taking it with vitamin E may increase its antioxidant and anti-inflammatory properties. Food sources include Brazil nuts, seafood, meat and poultry, cottage cheese and eggs, oats and brown rice. Vegetarians especially may benefit from a supplement of 200–400mcg daily combined with 400iu vitamin E (do not take more than the recommended dose).

Green essentials

The kitchen is home to a number of chemicals, including pesticides and formaldehyde, that can have adverse effects on health. It's easy to rid the home of potentially toxic household chemicals: simply clear out kitchen cupboards.

182

Kitchen chemical clearout

Pull out all the bottles of household cleaning fluids you can find in your house. Put to one side all those marked with the words "danger", "caution", "flammable" or "combustible" – these fluids contain potentially dangerous chlorine, ammonia or solvents. Add to the reject pile bottles featuring warnings not to use in unventilated spaces and certain temperatures, violently coloured products, and those that cause discomfort to eyes and nose when inhaled. For advice

on safe disposal call your household waste collector, or contact a local branch of Greenpeace or Friends of the Earth.

183

Dangerous surface wipes

Read the ingredients list for the cleaner you use to wipe over kitchen surfaces. Chemical names including the term "chlor" indicate a chlorinated substance. Chlorine is a hazardous air pollutant and may be neurotoxic and carcinogenic to mammals. Used over food-prep areas it can leave persistent residues that may transfer to food. Ditch it now and replace with an eco-cleaning fluid.

184
Avoid antibacterials

Adopt the example of Swedish hospitals and get rid of antimicrobial-impregnated chopping boards and sponges, sprays and hand-washing liquid. They are no more effective than soap and water and may contain biocides that accumulate in the environment and are suspected human carcinogens.

185
Green cleaners

Go shopping for green cleaners made from naturally derived surfactants (the main components of detergent) and biodegradable ingredients that have less impact on the environment, and so on the

health of our food and water. Ecover and Seventh Generation products are efficient, or make your own.

186
Non-toxic surface cleaner

Mix half and half water and distilled white vinegar in a pump spray. Add a squeeze of lemon juice for scent. Spray over surfaces and wipe away.

187
Instant tap cleaner

To make stainless steel features sparkle, wipe over with a paste made from half and half bicarbonate of soda and water. Wipe with a cloth.

188
Floor cleaner

Replace antibacterial floor cleaners with this water-based rinse. For stubborn stains, scrub first with natural liquid soap.

1 bucket very hot water
1 cup distilled white vinegar
8 drops essential oil of tea tree

Combine the water and vinegar in a mop bucket. Add the essential oil. Mop the floor, squeeze out the mop and repeat.

189
Miracle cloths

To avoid using detergent to erase grease and dirt, try a miracle microfibre cloth. Simply dampen and scrub.

190
Ban fresheners

Studies show air inside the home is two to five times more polluted than outdoor air. Don't add to it with artificial fragrances, especially those in block fragrances (they may contain camphor, linked with disorders of the nervous system). Avoid also aerosol air fresheners,

Home-made tap and surface cleaners are fragrant, effective and safe.

which propel VOCs (volatile organic compounds that are linked with neurological problems and depression) into the lungs, especially in steamy conditions.

191

Natural odour-eaters

Leave half a lemon in the kitchen or fridge to absorb ugly odours or rub a cut lemon over chopping boards and kitchen surfaces.

192

Air deodorizer

Place 4 drops of essential oil of citrus or lemongrass in the water bowl of a room vaporizer and light the candle or turn it on.

193

Kitchen spritzer

Add 8 drops essential oil of basil or geranium to water in a pump spray. Spritz into the air to disguise cooking smells, avoiding eyes and nose.

194

Grow tulips

Plant up tulip bulbs in the autumn to flower indoors in spring. They digest and neutralize xylene, ammonia and formaldehyde found in kitchen cleaning products. Or nurture a spider plant (*Chlorophytum elatum*) which thrives on carbon monoxide and formaldehyde.

195

Alternatives to plastic wrap

Avoid using cling-film, which may contain the plasticizing additive bisphenol-A, an oestrogen-mimicking chemical. Be especially wary of wrapping foods that are fatty, acidic or laced with alcohol in plastic: the food may absorb suspected hormone-disrupting and carcinogenic ingredients from the plastic. Fatty foods include dairy, meat, pastries and moist or topped cakes. Cover food with paper (not recycled paper towels which can contain flecks of metal). Don't reuse

packaging from one type of food for another: manufacturers only need ensure the packaging is safe for the food it is sold with. Instead wrap sandwiches and snacks in foil or greaseproof paper.

196

Safe storage

For refrigerator storage choose glass or ceramic containers with lids rather than plastic. Always avoid plastics with the recycling triangle marks 3, 6 or 7 (including bags) for food and drink storage.

197

Open a window

If you cook with gas, make sure the kitchen is well-ventilated (have a ventilation hood fitted or open a window or door) to avoid carbon monoxide poisoning. Good ventilation also cuts down on mould spores and minimizes harmful exposure to anti-mould paints and cleaning products.

Natural air fresheners: tulips, grown as indoor plants, absorb airborne toxins.

198
Cook in low-tox pans
Choose stainless steel or cast-iron pans coated in enamel, glass or terracotta. Avoid non-stick pans because once scratched, the coating can leach into food. One of the chemicals used in the manufacturing of these pans, perfluorooctanoic acid (PFOA), has been detected in the bodies of 92 per cent of Americans tested. This accumulates in brain tissue and can damage immunity.

199
Caring for terracotta
To preserve the life of terracotta pans, after washing dry well, then rub with olive oil.

200
Dishwasher safety
Don't open the dishwasher while still steamy: you risk inhaling THMs (trihalomethanes), suspected carcinogens created when chlorine in treated water reacts with organic matter and other chemicals.

201
Microwave safely
Transfer food into ceramic or heat-resistant glass cookware for microwaving. Some natural health therapists worry that microwaving plastic containers may cause packaging ingredients to migrate into food, especially high-fat foods. Some phthalate chemicals used to plasticize PVC food containers (avoid the recycling triangle mark 3) are known hormone disrupters and probable human carcinogens and are unstable in the plastic mix.

202
Have appliances serviced
Follow manufacturers' instructions on servicing appliances such as ovens, heating and hot water boilers. If gas flames and pilot lights burn orange rather than blue call a gas technician immediately.

203
Debugging organic greens
Discard the outer leaves, pull off the remaining leaves and leave to soak in water for 10 minutes. Place in a colander under cold running water, making sure each leaf is washed well. Use a centrifugal spinner to remove excess water. If you choose to buy ready-to-eat salad leaves, wash before using (a soak in cold water also perks up tired leaves).

204
Washing root vegetables
Soak dirty organic vegetables in plenty of water. Scrub with a brush to loosen ingrained soil, then rinse under running water.

Debug organic greens thoroughly, washing them in a colander under running water.

205
Storing olive oil
Buy olive oil in opaque glass bottles and cap tightly after use. Antioxidant phenols retain more potency when unexposed to light and air. Store in a cool place, since they are also destroyed by heat.

206
Reduce your toxic load
Persistent chemicals in the environment enter our bodies from mattresses and sofas and essential electrical goods in the home. Some chemicals never fully break down, "bioaccumulating" within body fat. They are known to interfere with hormones, and have been linked with memory and immune system problems, and even cancer. Reduce exposure by choosing organic mattresses and naturally flame-retardant sofas, and always look for electrical goods marked "safer".

2 Rejuvenating exercise

Regular exercise is the key to healthy muscles, bones and body systems. Physical training plays an essential role in anti-ageing stress-busting: people who exercise report better mood and more energy than those who don't, and they suffer less insomnia and stress-related symptoms. And at this time of changing body shape, exercise bolsters self-confidence as you see muscles become toned, posture lift, stamina, flexibility and range of motion increase. Exercise also helps keep the brain functioning in a youthful way, by boosting circulation and right-left brain coordination. Mentally challenging activities, from bridge to Sudoku, exercise the memory and build connections between brain cells that help keep your reasoning sharp.

Working the body

By strengthening muscles and bones as the body ages, exercise sustains good posture, bone density and joint mobility, which in turn keeps you active and able to exercise – a positive spiral. And by boosting the efficiency of the cardiovascular system (heart and lungs), exercise helps every part of the body function efficiently.

207

How often?

Aim for at least 30 minutes of moderate physical activity most days of the week (at least five). To prevent weight gain, you might need to boost that time slot to 60 minutes. Two of those sessions should incorporate weight training (see Nos. 338–49). If you find it hard to make a full hour available, breaking sessions down into 10-minute time bands doesn't seem to reduce the health benefits.

208

When not to exercise

Consult your doctor before beginning an exercise programme, especially if you have a medical condition, back, muscle or joint problems, mobility limitations or are exercising for the first time. Always tell exercise instructors about health problems. If you feel under the weather, have a fever or are coming down with flu don't

exercise. After a cold or flu allow time for recovery before returning to the gym, and take it easy for the first few sessions. Don't try to work through injury: take your level of training right down for a couple of weeks or until you see improvement.

209

Work with your doctor

Many family doctors prescribe exercise instead of medication as the first round of treatment for certain chronic health conditions. Ask your doctor about exercise programmes run in association with a local gym or sports club.

210

Build up slowly

Harness the enthusiasm to become superfit when it strikes, but don't launch wholeheartedly into hardcore aerobics sessions right away. If you are new to exercise, it might be better to search out a class specifically designed for older

people – yoga or aqua fitness is a good place to start – and to take things easy, working to a level at which you feel comfortable. You can train to run a marathon or learn the headstand, but build up to it slowly.

211

Time to enjoy

Some people like to jumpstart the day with a swim or early-bird yoga class. Others prefer to exercise in the late afternoon or early evening, when muscles are more supple, joints less creaky and coordination better. Find a time that suits you: the more you enjoy working out, the more likely it is that you will keep to your fitness resolutions.

212

Work benefits

Find out if your workplace offers fitness facilities or discounts on gym membership. Many employees fail to use these perks simply because they don't know about them.

213

Active leisure

Plan family time and business networking around physical activity. If you spend Saturday morning swimming or playing tennis with kids and one evening a week bowling or learning to jive with colleagues, everyone gains.

214
Exercise outdoors

It can be joyous to exercise outdoors – a boost for spirit as well as body. The feel-good buzz after exercising in nature leaves you feeling exhilarated, yet grounded and calm. Whenever possible, find an excuse to go jogging at dawn, swim in the ocean or practise yoga in the garden (upward-facing poses take on another dimension when you stare at the sky). Find a t'ai chi class that practises regularly in a park: gain courage from numbers.

215
Four-stage workout

For an effective workout make sure your exercise sessions include four main elements: a gentle warm-up followed by aerobic or cardiovascular exercise to work the heart and lungs, weight-bearing exercises to strengthen muscles and bones, and finally a cool down stretch and relaxation.

216
Don't rush

Don't be anxious to speed through to the part of an exercise programme you believe does you most good: sit-ups perhaps or yoga back bends. It might be more useful for your muscles, joints and commitment to spend a good amount of time in relaxation at the start of a yoga class releasing tense parts of the body towards the floor, or to devote adequate time to warming up in preparation for cardio work.

217
Take breaks

If you exercise regularly, don't be afraid to take time out for holidays and illness. Make sure you have one day of rest each week. Sometimes having a break allows us insights into new ways of working, and builds up enthusiasm when we feel jaded. If you are training very hard, for a marathon perhaps, be aware that you run the risk of depleting your immune system. In one study people who ran the Los Angeles marathon were six times more susceptible to a cold or flu than those who exercised regularly but didn't run the race.

Exercising outdoors brings with it a calming fix of nature.

218
Keep hydrated

It's important to keep hydrated during exercise as you get older. Even if you drink the recommended eight glasses of water a day, drink more after taking sweaty exercise to replace lost fluids.

219
When there's no time

If you feel you do not have enough time to exercise, try writing a schedule, blocking out time in your diary for fitness sessions as you would for a work meeting or doctor's appointment. Consider that time sacred and don't allow anything to eat into it. You owe it to yourself, your family and your job to be good-natured, efficient and focused, and exercise brings all these benefits.

220
Warning signs

Stop exercising and seek medical advice if you suffer any of the following symptoms:
- chest pain
- back or pelvic pain
- shortness of breath (mild breathlessness is good)
- headaches and dizziness
- muscle weakness or extreme fatigue
- difficulty walking
- calf pain or swelling

Which exercise?

The most effective way to ensure you work out consistently is to choose activities that make you feel positive and confident about yourself, and to train in a place convenient to home or work. If you struggle to keep up with your class or you have to travel miles, you find you run out of the willpower you need to drag yourself off the sofa.

Dance for body, brain and zest.

221
Taste first

If you don't find a form of exercise that suits you, you won't stick with it. Try a few taster sessions before signing up to a course of lessons.

222
Be daring

Try a new activity once a month: if you enjoy dance, try a ballet workshop, or go for something completely not you, such as tag rugby. Dare yourself to try a sport you enjoy watching but have never plucked up courage to do – surfing or skating, trampolining or climbing.

223
Go with the seasons

Keep the mind alert by varying activities with the seasons. Enjoy outdoor exercise on light summer evenings: find a tennis partner or join a softball team. In winter, cosset yourself in a cosy yoga class or warm up with an intimate salsa session.

224
Dance for joie de vivre

Bollywood to belly-dancing, samba to tango, line dancing to ass-shaking street styles, dancing is the way to exercise without knowing you're exercising. Learning and executing steps and working to complex rhythms exercises brain as well as muscles, and posture awareness becomes second nature.

225
Classes for company
If you are the kind of person who can always find an excuse not to exercise, organized classes might suit you best. Having others ready to drag you along might also help – organize a group from the office to attend classes so you can't opt out.

226
T'ai chi to oil the joints
With its controlled, gentle and continuous movements, t'ai chi is particularly good if you aren't as mobile as you once were, since it builds muscle and bone strength without putting pressure on the joints. It benefits the brain and mood by focusing and calming mind and body, and its rebalancing breathing techniques offer insight into how we breathe when we move. Learn with a well-trained teacher.

227
Yoga for everyone
Whatever your stage of life, yoga is the perfect form of exercise for mind and body, and it's never too late to start. As well as the obvious physical benefits (improving posture, boosting circulation, promoting balance and coordination, strengthening core muscles), yoga helps you stop and focus within, which is both stress-busting and energizing. It sheds light on other areas of life, such as emotions and relationships, that might need work. It also teaches breath-control techniques to calm, focus and rebalance body and mind.

228
Choose your type
Iyengar yoga is the best starting point if you would like a structured grounding in the poses with close teacher supervision. If you prefer a challenging cardio and strength workout, look for Ashtanga or power yoga, Bikram or hot yoga, or vinyasa classes that teach flowing sequences of poses. To explore the spiritual side of yoga, try Sivananda or Kundalini yoga. Hatha yoga classes often offer a mix of approaches.

229
Yoga as therapy
Yoga may be effective for numerous health conditions, ranging from back pain and depression to carpal tunnel syndrome and arthritis. If you have a health condition, find a yoga therapy teacher who will set out a programme of postures and breathing exercises specially tailored to your condition.

230
Try Pilates
Pilates classes suit those who don't enjoy sweaty forms of exercise, people with injuries and those keen to maintain good posture with age. The movements are very low

There is a yoga class to suit every personality type.

impact – you might find them imperceptible at first – and focus on strengthening core muscles in the centre of the body that support the spine and pelvis. Breathing techniques enhance the moves. Pilates is effective at increasing mobility, developing core strength and flexibility, achieving good body alignment and helping prevent back problems. It also instils a sense of discipline and understanding of how the body moves, ensuring flowing movement continues as we age.

Swimming tones and strengthens, relaxes and energizes.

231
Go swimming for mobility

Supportive but resistant, relaxing yet energizing, water is the ideal medium in which to exercise safely the heart and lungs, muscles and bones. Aim for a 20-minute swim 3–6 times a week. Water exercise is especially beneficial if you have aching joints: buoyant water supports body weight, reducing the strain on vulnerable areas such as knees and hips. Water resistance makes for effective toning and strengthening, especially of thigh and chest muscles. It also soothes puffy legs as water pressure encourages the movement of fluids back into the bloodstream, reducing swelling. Swimming promotes deep, controlled breathing and studies show that exercising in water boosts the immune system.

232
Water fitness

If you can't swim confidently but want to share the benefits of exercising supported by water, take a walk in a calm ocean or try an aqua aerobic class in the shallow end of a pool. In studies women who exercise in water have reduced heart rates and blood pressure compared with those who exercise on land.

233
Walk for strength

Walking is not just good for maintaining bone density, it can be as good for the heart as jogging, suggests a small study. Brisk walking, covering 1½–2 miles a week, can reduce the risk of developing cardiovascular disease. Aim for this modest distance when you start walking, building on it to gain even more health benefits as fitness and self-confidence increase.

234
Take a hike

All you need for walking outdoors is a pair of walking boots. Walking off road brings extra benefits because as the terrain changes you have to adjust your posture and vary the muscles used, which also stimulates the brain. Warm up with slow strides then speed up gradually, pumping your arms. Once warm, alternate short steps and long strides, tackle inclines and introduce interval training – 10 steps jogging followed by 10 steps walking.

235

Train to run a marathon

The average age for competitors in the London marathon is 39. Many older people embark upon a half or full marathon as an opportunity to prove to themselves and others that life truly does begin at 40, 50 or more. Completing the course is a great way to boost self-confidence when your peer group is struggling with mid-life crises. If you are raising money for charity while you run, it makes your personal challenge all the more meaningful.

236

Rowing for good posture

Working out on water can be a source of sheer pleasure, especially in the early morning. Seek out a rowing club or kayak classes at your local pool or reservoir. Rowing is great for building strength while the body is supported and insists on good posture, which conditions the core muscles and works the heart and lungs.

237

Racquet sports for reaction times

Tennis, badminton and squash enhance coordination and reaction times and are a tonic for the brain, since it's disadvantageous to your game to zone out while playing.

Apart from the obvious benefits for heart and lungs, agility and strength, belonging to a sports club is a boost to your psychological health since most welcome members to a range of social activities.

238

Cycling to get around

Exercise the heart and lungs while supporting the joints on a stationary bike as you watch TV or let your cycle be a means of transport. Don a helmet, gloves and fluorescent clothing and appreciate how liberating it is to be freed from bus timetables and traffic jams. Don't worry over much about inhaling pollutants – the health benefits of cycling outweigh the risks.

239

Look into local fitness classes

If you prefer to exercise with a teacher up front demonstrating what you need to do, join a fitness class at your local gym. Read the gym prospectus in advance to find out which classes suit your level of fitness: general toning classes for legs, bum and tum can be quite gentle, as can some classes involving fitness balls. Others, such as spinning, circuit training, boxing training and cardio step, might require a good level of muscle strength and stamina. It's a good idea to have a word with the instructor if you are not sure which class suits you.

Don a cycling helmet and go wherever your bike takes you.

Exercising the brain

From the mid-20s, brain function starts to decline, although you may not notice this until decades later. New learning experiences help stop the rot by strengthening and extending the connections (and networks) in the brain that enable us to store memories and stay sharp. However bad your memory is now, mental aerobics, good nutrition and moderate physical activity can improve thinking and memory skills.

Do crosswords to challenge mental agility.

240
Cook with sage
Sage is traditionally associated with improving memory. Research has shown that people who take sage oil in capsule form before memory tests perform better than those who take a placebo. The purple variety is best – use it to flavour roasts and sauces or make a cup of surprisingly drinkable tea (see No. 931).

241
Take ginkgo
The herb *Ginkgo biloba* has earned its reputation as a brain tonic because it has a beneficial effect on the

peripheral blood circulation, improving blood supply to the brain. (It helps with piles and varicose veins for the same reason.) Gingko is prescribed to dementia patients in France and Germany. Take as a herbal extract or tincture as prescribed by your herbalist or following instructions on the pack. Avoid if taking other medication.

242
Switch hands
Use your "wrong" hand to manipulate the mouse, brush teeth and hair and open doors. This expands the circuits in the part of the brain that processes that hand.

243
Everyday mental challenges
Get into the habit of tackling a crossword or Sudoku puzzle most days. One study found that people who complete a crossword four times a week appeared to reduce their risk of dementia by 47 per cent.

244
Rearrange familiar objects
Move objects you habitually reach for without thinking in the morning: alarm clock, toothbrush, cutlery, breakfast cereal. This forces your brain to shift into gear early on and may make mornings more wakeful.

Use sage leaves to flavour food and boost memory.

245

Become a lifelong student

Continuing study through each new decade keeps the brain performing in a youthful way. Book an adult education course (to maintain interest make it a subject you feel passionate about), join a book group or local history society, a choir with a challenging and changing repertoire or try something practical such as car maintenance.

The group aspect is important because socializing keeps the memory sharp and brain agile.

246

Learn a language

Enrol in a language school or invest in a course to follow in the car or on the train. Learning languages stimulates the frontal lobes, the part of the brain that functions less efficiently as we age. Book a holiday in a country that speaks your chosen language and download some local information. With a dictionary, pick through the weather report, arts reviews and events guides.

247

Build up to daily meditation

Find 10 to 20 minutes a day to sit quietly. Researchers found that daily meditation may slow age-related brain deterioration by

248

Holy fig tree pose

Balancing postures in yoga require you to find a focus point and maintain concentration on it. This not only helps you find and explore your centre of gravity to prevent falls, but also enhances memory skills.

1 Stand tall, feet hip-width apart. Step forward with your right foot. Straighten your left leg and lift it behind you, keeping your hips level.

2 If you feel steady lift your right arm overhead, your fingers pulling upward and your shoulder dropping away from your ear.

3 Lift your left arm 45° to the side, stretching fingertips. Look forward, and visualize each limb stretching on its own plane. Repeat on other side.

altering the physical structure of the brain. People who meditated for 40 minutes a day had a more dense cerebral cortex than people who did not. In other studies, practitioners of Transcendental Meditation demonstrated cognitive, perceptual and physical abilities equivalent to people up to 10 years their junior.

249
Basic meditating
Set an alarm to ring in five minutes. Sit with your spine upright, feet flat on the floor, palms resting on thighs.

Relax your shoulders and jaw and switch off from everyday concerns. Close your eyes.

Focus on your breath moving in and out. Let this steer you away from trains of thought. If it helps, breathe in to a count of three or four. Exhale to the same count. When distractions arise, focus on your counting or awareness of your flow of breath in and out.

Return to regular breathing as the alarm rings and slowly open your eyes. Once you feel easy with the technique, increase meditation time in increments of 5 minutes.

Close friends are important for emotional wellbeing.

250
Enjoy family and friends
Make time to enjoy the company of friends and family. In one study of older people, those with emotional support from a strong social network were more likely to retain memory, abstract thinking and language skills, even if the relationships were testing!

251
Scent your day
Perfume various times of day with different aromas to establish associations that trigger new neural pathways. Scent the car with 2 drops of essential oil of basil. Follow your morning shower with a distinctly scented body oil (see Nos. 612–18).

252
Holiday senses
Choose a new scented soap for a holiday or weekend away. This will stimulate memories of your break when you use it again at home.

253
Eat greens
Consume foods containing plant antioxidants, such as spinach and blueberries. An American study suggests this helps reverse mental decline as we age. Plants that are also rich in folate are even better: researchers found older men who

Iron-rich eggs, oily fish and pulses help prevent memory loss through anaemia.

ate folate-rich leafy greens and citrus fruit had significantly less age-related decline in memory and brain function over three years than those whose diets were low in folate.

254
Dine on fish
Eating fish at least once a week can slow the rate of cognitive decline in older people by up to 13 per cent per year, reports one study. Other research suggests omega-3 fatty acids in oily fish are vital for the functioning of brain-cell receptors. Eat different varieties – mackerel, sardines and organically farmed trout – two or three times a week.

255
Include iron
Anaemia may cloud the memory with age because iron helps transport oxygen to the brain. For iron, eat red meat, poultry, fish and eggs, and if vegetarian, plenty of pulses, nuts, seeds and whole grains, dark leafy greens, apricots and dark chocolate. For maximum absorption, accompany with a source of vitamin C, such as freshly squeezed orange juice, and the B vitamins found in yeast extract.

256
Zinc for thinking
Zinc helps us think (find it in meat, poultry, fish, nuts, seeds, whole grains and onions). Absorption is blocked by a large intake of iron so monitor your zinc intake diligently if you have an iron-rich diet.

257
Care about choline
In a study of adults over 50, a five-week supplement of choline halved memory lapse. This mineral aids the absorption and use of good fats, vital for cell membranes, and helps the transmission of signals across nerve endings in the brain's networks. Add meat, nuts and eggs into your diet daily.

258
Try stimulating teas
Incorporate new herbal teas into your day. Lemon balm seems to help the brain store and retrieve information. Green and black tea are associated with preventing memory loss with age. Peppermint tea stimulates the brain, promoting concentration and alertness.

259
Unplug the phone
The constant ping of emails and interruption of phone calls can cause IQ to drop by 10 points found a study commissioned by Hewlett-Packard, leading to loss of concentration and problem-solving skills. Unplug the phone and resist the temptation to

check emails for two-hour runs when you need to achieve results. Get up and walk across the office to talk to people instead, which also counts towards your daily activity quotient.

260

Play games

Games such as chess and draughts that force you to think ahead, plan alternative strategies and pre-guess others' moves are very valuable. They also advance spatial awareness (useful for reading maps).

261

Change tack

Get outdoors for a walk to boost circulation to the brain when you have a problem to solve. Switch off and turn your focus to your surroundings with your nose, ears and sense of touch. Walk backwards and sideways to forge new circuits in the brain. After 15 minutes, start your return journey. Now ponder potential solutions.

262

Mall strolling

Research with older adults shows that brisk walking in indoor malls is a valuable addition to the 30 minutes a day exercise rule. See if a mall near you runs a walking scheme for year-round socializing to keep the brain sharp.

Exercise essentials

Getting kitted out with the right pair of shoes or specialist equipment for your chosen activity helps you relax and feel comfortable. This helps boost your motivation to keep exercising, and so raise the amount of physical activity in your daily life, leading to more muscle, denser bones, healthier organs and increased energy.

263

Comfortable clothes

Choose garments loose enough to permit a good range of movement (in particular avoid restrictive waistbands, shoulder straps and under-wired bras), yet not so baggy that they catch on limbs or fall off when you bend over. Women engaging in jogging and other jerky movements might feel more comfortable in a sports bra. Layers are vital for sports in which you start cold then get hot. Choose pure wool base layers for dryness and comfort.

264

The right shoes are essential

You need the right shoes for whichever activity you choose. For activities involving jogging, running or jumping, choose training shoes with cushioning and other built-in features to support the spine (some shoes have cushioning specially positioned for beginning runners). Ask advice at a specialist sports shop (rather than a fashion sneaker store); even better, shop at a gym selling sports equipment.

Choose the right shoes for your activity: what's suitable for an aerobics class won't suit t'ai chi.

Yoga mats should have a sticky finish to prevent slipping.

265

Suitable socks

Appropriate socks are important: some running socks have mesh sections for air circulation and are seam-free to prevent blisters. Try outdoors or extreme-sports stores for socks with cushioning and in a range of performance fabrics.

266

Changing room courage

If communal changing rooms make you feel anxious, put on exercise gear beneath regular clothes before you go or choose sessions at a quiet time of day. Do a tour of all the local sports centres to find a place where you feel comfortable. As you become more addicted to the endorphin high that follows a good exercise session you might feel less concerned.

267

Love your yoga mat

Buy a real yoga mat (not a camping mat) with a sticky finish to prevent palms and soles slipping away from each other in postures such as downward dog and triangle-based legwork. Support should be so effortless that you forget you're on a mat. Mats that retain the outline of feet when you step away are useful for checking alignment. Make sure the mat can be machine washed without disintegrating. Choose a colour you love: the more attached you are to your yoga mat, the more you'll want to put in practice hours.

268

Take a towel

If you're prone to perspiring, take a towel along to your exercise class. Use it to wipe brow and hands (to prevent slipping) or as a hygienic layer if you have to lie on shared mats. A rolled-up towel can be useful to cushion bony parts of the body when working on a yoga mat, or to provide support beneath sitting bones or heels in certain postures.

269

Blocks and bolsters

Yoga foam or, even better, cork blocks help you into poses you could not otherwise achieve. They are used in some types of yoga not only by beginners, but by experienced practitioners to achieve lift, opening or support that allows a student to extend further, reach higher, or sink more effectively. Don't buy them before you start a class; see what the teacher advises (various schools of yoga have different thoughts about their use) and try a selection of thicknesses and shapes in class to see which you prefer. Some poses call for the cushioning of a firm bolster.

270

Fitness balls

Some forms of fitness training are based around a large inflated ball. Sit on it to practise balancing, lie over it prone or supine for sit-ups, back extensions and press-ups. Or lie on the floor raising legs against the ball

Fitness balls can be fun, but learn how to use them from a trained instructor.

to isolate action in one set of muscles and prevent larger, more often used muscle groups taking over. Do attend a class to learn the basics with a trained instructor, as balls are fun but can be challenging to stay on.

271

Bands and belts

Flexible bands might be called for in toning classes in place of hand weights to provide enough resistance for an effective bicep curl or side raise. Don't buy your own until you've tested them out in class and know how they work. Buckled fabric belts are used in yoga to help students into poses, for instance when unable to reach toes or keep legs in a crossed position. They are extremely effective.

272

Blankets

Always take a blanket to yoga. It's useful to cushion ankles, knees and hips in sitting and prone postures and is essential for final relaxation, when you lie on your back without moving for up to 10 minutes. The body cools quickly when motionless, so covering yourself with a blanket is vital in winter and in cold studios. Being covered up adds to the sense of retreating within to find inner calm – you may find you don't want to emerge at the end of the session.

Keeping motivated

If you aren't naturally sporty you may find the lure of the TV, bath or bar too strong to keep up an effective exercise regime. A range of actions may help, from recruiting a friend to accompany you on jogging sessions or fitness classes to plotting your progress in a diary.

273

Enlist a friend

Working out with a buddy is one of the best ways of maintaining motivation, but don't let your relationship become competitive. Each of us has a different exercise history, body type and levels of mental and physical stamina. We also all have differing requirements and expectations of an exercise regime. If you find your exercise partner is making you feel disheartened because she can stretch further or hit harder than you, then it is probably time to find a new partner.

274

Solitary thought

Some people prefer to exercise alone, so they are better able to switch off and enjoy exercise almost as a form of meditation. If that applies to you, you might prefer jogging or swimming, walking or

Maintain motivation by working out with a friend.

Mysore-style self-practise yoga rather than a jolly band of badminton players.

275
Women-only sessions

Seek out women-only mornings or evenings to avoid having to face rows of sweaty young muscle men in the gym (unless that's part of the attraction). Being surrounded by people like you rather than young exercise fiends in tight-fitting lycra can prevent motivation slipping away. Women-only evenings also often offer attractive add-ons, such as free use of the sauna or steam room or a complimentary swim.

276
Set realistic goals

Don't expect to see impressive results instantly. Although it can help motivation to choose an activity in which you can see progression relatively quickly, it's good to keep fitness expectations realistic. Talk to gym staff about drawing up personal fitness targets, and ask for help in monitoring them. If you join an exercise class with fewer than 10 members and a regular teacher, the teacher should be able to push you towards a path that's right for you. If you don't feel you're getting on, splurge on a session with a personal trainer to discuss and establish realistic expectations.

277
Keep an exercise diary

To chart progress, fill in an exercise diary. Don't try to see progression with every exercise session – this can be too dispiriting – but every month make a list of the things you can do that you weren't able to before. Each small change signals a more youthful you.

278
Online communities

It can help to join an online community of exercisers, especially if you are training for a national event, such as a charity fun run or a marathon. Online you'll find progressive training plans, trouble-shooting tips and advice from expert coaches, and you'll be able to moan to, enthuse and egg on fellow exercisers on message boards.

279
Think yourself active

If you think of yourself as an active person who exercises you are more likely to become one, a study suggests. If you've lived a largely sedentary life until now, this mind-shift may take some getting used to. It can help to join a club of active people, who naturally include you in their fitness activities. Affirmations are helpful, too: start repeating to yourself "I am active and fit".

Women-only classes may be the answer if you feel intimidated by a gym full of men.

280
Expect to succeed

Those who expect health to decline with age are less likely to be physically active researchers have found. Keep your expectations of good health high and you are more likely to stay active and mobile regardless of age.

281
Motivation tip

Although older people tend to get exhausted more quickly by physical tasks than people in their 20s and 30s, researchers have found that older people who exercise regularly progress their fitness levels more quickly than younger co-exercisers.

Build exercise into life

If exercising at the gym is just another chore you don't have the energy or enthusiasm to keep up, squeeze opportunities for exercise into your home and work life. Walk don't drive, use stairs in preference to lifts and take a brisk stroll at lunchtime. Spend weekends working in the garden. Harness the urge to spring clean or clutter-clear, scrubbing floors and painting walls to keep fit, and enjoy the feel-good mood that comes when endorphins are released by exercise.

Dog walking is a great anti-ageing tonic.

Double action: practise pliés at the bathroom sink while cleaning your teeth.

282

Stand up

Simply stand more to gain health benefits: researchers at the Mayo Clinic found that obese people sit for two and a half hours longer a day than those who are leaner.

283

Toothbrush plié

Think about how you can build exercises into your daily routines. For example, here's how to work the thighs and buttocks by doing a plié while cleaning your teeth.
Take a good step to the side, angling your feet outwards. Hold the basin lightly for support and balance, if necessary.
As you exhale, draw your tummy muscles towards your spine. As you inhale, lengthen your torso. On the next exhalation bend your knees over your toes. Hold for a few seconds, pulling up your pelvic floor muscles.
Inhaling, straighten your legs back to the starting position. Repeat up to 12 times. Build up to three sets.

284

Walking the dog

If you are a dog owner, you have no choice but to exercise every day. Dog walking is a great anti-ageing tonic, since it also involves socializing with other owners.

285

Active commuting

Get off your bus or train one stop early and walk the rest of the journey. When the walk becomes easily do-able (as fitness levels improve), get off a stop earlier. Over a few weeks build up to a 20-minute walk before reaching work.

286

Travel meditation

In Zen Buddhism zazen, "just sitting", is a form of meditation in itself. Try it on the train or bus. Sit upright, palms on thighs. Soften your gaze, looking forwards and down. Focus inside and follow your breath. Watch thoughts and sensations as an observer, aware of but disinterested in them.

287

Make the most of lunchtime

Get outdoors every day for a brisk lunchtime stroll. A Canadian study suggests people who walk for 30 minutes at a time burn more fat and have lower tension levels than those who exercise in shorter bursts.

288

Up your pace

Increase your pace when walking. Award yourself a point for every person you overtake and deduct one for anyone who overtakes you. Within reason, set yourself a higher tally target each week.

289

Using stairs

When you first walk up the stairs at work, in department stores and in subways notice how your heart and breathing race. After using stairs regularly for a few weeks, chart your progress – your breathing will be less ragged and your heart pound less.

290

Start fidgeting

Research shows that fidgeters who move around a great deal, tapping toes, walking to the water cooler and pacing while they think tend to lead more active lives and are leaner as a result. Cultivate a few fidgets.

291

Chores as exercise

Energetic car washing forms a valuable part of a home exercise regime. Work at a continual pace until slightly out of breath, stretching, scrubbing, carrying and pitching buckets of water. Vacuuming adds value when sustained over 10 minutes or more. Use the pectoral muscles in your chest when manoeuvring upright cleaners, paying attention to good posture and engaging core abdominal muscles.

292

Creating space

Set aside a dedicated space at home for exercise and meditation. Choose a quiet sanctuary where you feel comfortable and confident. Clear

away clutter, then sweep or mop –
add 2–3 drops of essential oil of
lemon grass or eucalyptus to final
rinse water to quicken the senses.

293
Gardening for fitness

Half an hour's vigorous gardening –
digging, mowing, carrying watering
cans, forking sacks of manure –
counts as one exercise session.

294
Turn off the TV

On average people spend four hours
daily in front of the TV. Aim to
employ your leisure time more
actively to contribute to your daily
30 minutes' exercise. At home
declare non-TV days – throw a
cover over the set if needs be.

295
Ad-break squat

Strengthen abdominals and thighs
by standing with head, shoulders
and buttocks pressed against a wall,
feet a foot or so in front, hip-width
apart. Bend your knees and slide
down the wall a little. Exhaling,
contract your abdominal muscles
and tilt your pelvis so your lower
back presses against the wall. If you
can't see your knees when you look
down, exhale and descend until you
can. Aim to hold, breathing evenly,
until the end of the ad break.

296
Doorpost stretch

If you habitually hunch
forward, collapsing the chest,
you prevent a full intake of
anti-ageing oxygen with each
in-breath. As an antidote,
stand in a doorway. Place
your palms and forearms on
the door jamb on each side.
Without moving your arms,
push your chest forward, and
step one foot through the
door arch. Feel an energizing
stretch across the chest.

Active in the office

Muscles that stay in the same position for long hours – as they do when you work at your desk without a break – eventually weaken and become prone to injury as the body ages. Stretching at your desk helps keep the muscles limber and boosts your productivity by increasing circulation to the brain for a wake-up effect and a shot of feel-good hormones.

297
Sticky reminder

Stick a note on your desk or computer reminding you to take a break every 20 minutes. Take a few minutes to walk around and stretch.

298
Wrist recovery

After a period of mouse use, circle your wrists inwards, then outwards. Try to keep the rest of your forearm stationary. Holding your left fingers with your right palm, left palm facing upwards, stretch your left arm away, pushing through the wrist and pulling your fingers towards your elbow. Repeat on the other arm.

299
Shoulder rolls

When neck and shoulders feel tense, for instance after holding a phone in the crook of your neck, scrunch your shoulders up to your ears. Squeeze tightly and hold. Exhaling,

Don't forget to take a break from your computer every 20 minutes.

let everything go, sighing. Repeat three or four times, then roll your shoulders very slowly up, back and down. Reverse the action.

300
Lunchtime lie-down

Take every opportunity to lie on your front if you work at a desk. Go to the park at lunchtime and lie with legs hip-width apart. Bend your arms and rest your forehead on your hands. If you can, let your heels flop inwards. Consciously release

tension in the lower back. Imagine the pelvic area becoming warm, heavy and sinking into soft sand, aches and pains dissolving. Feel your breath in your belly, pressing against the support of the ground.

301
Desk roll-down

To release tension in the neck, shoulders and lower back, sit tall with feet flat on the floor, arms dangling from the shoulder joints. Exhaling, let the weight of your head bring your chin towards your chest. Keep rolling down extremely slowly, allowing your shoulders to droop forward. Come to rest with eyes on knees, arms hanging heavily, palms on the floor. Roll up very slowly on inhalations.

302
After-work release

Lie on your back, legs hip-width apart, knees bent, feet flat on the floor, arms by your side. Lift your toes, splay, then replace.

Inhaling, imagine breathing into the back of your pelvis. Feel everything soften. Exhale and relax your pelvis towards the floor.

Inhaling, feel your upper back widen and soften. Exhaling, let your shoulder blades melt into the floor. Lengthen the back of the neck. Feel your head, pelvis and feet supported by the floor.

303
Seated side bend

The sides of the torso rarely lengthen in everyday activities yet need to do so to maintain good posture. Sit tall on a supportive chair, feet flat on the floor, tailbone weighted heavily on the chair. Exhaling, draw your abdominal muscles towards your lower back. Inhaling, slowly lengthen your left side, growing out of the pelvis and into your underarm. Let your right arm and shoulder drop towards the floor. When you feel your lower back engage stop. Inhaling, come back to centre and repeat on the other side.

304
Seated rotation

To slow loss of spinal mobility with age, rotate the spine daily. It recharges vital energy, helping to relieve lower back pain and digestive ills. Sit tall facing forward, feet flat on the floor. Exhaling, turn your entire trunk to face left. Anchor in your right buttock to keep the pelvis facing forward. When you have twisted as far as comfort allows, turn your head to look over your left shoulder. With each inhalation let your spine grow up from its base to the crown of your head. With exhalations, see if you can gently turn further from the base of the spine. Come back to centre on an inhalation. Rotate to the other side.

Maintaining posture

Good posture is the essence of a young-looking body. Aligning the joints dissolves tension in the shoulders and lower back, allows your spine to find its full range of motion, promotes easier breathing and defines your figure, helping you look trimmer and more self-confident. Good posture also prevents neck problems, exercises the abdominal and pelvic muscles, protects your back as you lift and carry and makes fitness workouts more effective.

305
Check yourself

Poor posture can lead to backache and a stiff neck and shoulders, not to mention a stooped profile. Stiff areas aren't used and so become stiffer, other body parts taking over to compensate, leading to imbalances and problems with flexibility and strength. Check your posture at regular intervals, perhaps when you stop at a red light or on the hourly news report. Stretch, shake out tension and restack the vertebrae.

306
Sitting posture

On a chair, imagine your tailbone is dropping heavily onto the seat behind you. This helps bring your spine into neutral. Let the crown of your head float towards the ceiling; tuck the chin in slightly to keep the neck long. Visualize space between each vertebra.

307
Against the wall

Sit cross-legged with your lower back touching a wall. Anchor your legs and buttocks to the floor. Inhaling, feel your spine grow out of your hips. Breathing out, draw your abdominal muscles back. On your next inhalation, rest both shoulder blades against the wall. Visualize the crown of your head growing taller.

308
Adjust your chair

Choose an adjustable office chair. Move the seat until both feet are flat on the floor, legs hip-width apart, knees over ankles, backs of thighs well supported. Adjust the back of the seat to support your lower back with shoulders balanced over hips, ears aligned with the shoulders. Position the monitor so that you face forward. Keep elbows at right angles to upper arms, shoulders relaxed.

309
Look in the mirror
Look at how you're standing. Does one hip jut forward? Is all your body weight balanced on one foot? Is one shoulder higher or does your head tilt to one side? Which parts of your body look tense? How are your shoulders, jaw, chest and stomach?

310
While you wait
Practise standing well at the supermarket checkout, while waiting for a bus or at the water cooler. Stand with feet hip-width apart, outside edges parallel. Shift your bodyweight so it is equal between both feet: sway from side to side and forwards and back to test your balance. Centre your hips over your knees. Draw your abdominal muscles back and bring your buttocks together without gripping. Extend from hips to armpits equally on both sides. Broaden your chest, relax your shoulders, keeping them centred over your hips, and lift through the back of the neck.

311
Walking tall
To improve your posture as you walk, lift your gaze from the ground and look a good way in front of you, fixing your eyes on objects at eye level. Think about your weight staying behind you, so your back foot is heavy and front foot light. As you walk imagine objects coming towards you rather than you moving towards them, as if standing on a moving walkway at an airport.

312

Imagine a balloon ...

Whenever you feel old and saggy, imagine a helium-filled balloon is tied to the crown of your head. Feel it elongating the vertebrae at the back of the neck. Look forward.

313

Pilates neutral pelvis

Finding a neutral (natural) position for the pelvis is one of the first lessons of Pilates. Lie on your back with knees bent, in line with your hips, feet flat on the floor a comfortable distance from your buttocks. Place the heels of your hands on your hip bones, fingers on your pubic bone. Tilt your pelvis up, so your lower back presses into the ground. Then roll your pelvis under so your lower back arches away from the floor. Now try to find a middle place, between flexion and extension, where your hip and pubic bones (and hands) are level. This is neutral. Practise lying, standing and sitting in neutral.

314

Try the Alexander Technique

This therapy re-educates the body away from mental and physical habits that over time can lead to back pain and aggravate stress-related symptoms, repetitive strain and other injuries. Work with a teacher to learn the precise instructions and experience a subtle, hands-on manipulation and balance-adjustment that helps you feel lighter, move more easily and elegantly and look slimmer.

315

Pelvic lift

Pelvic muscles weaken with age, especially after the menopause. To guard against stress incontinence, do pelvic floor, or Kegel, exercises (see No. 350) daily for the rest of your life. This is vital if you have had children (especially after three or more vaginal deliveries).

316

Locating core muscles

Muscles deep within the abdomen and pelvis support the spine against gravity like a corset, stabilizing and protecting youthful posture. To locate these core muscles, sit upright, feet flat on the floor. Exhaling, draw your abdominal muscles back, as if taking your navel towards your lower back. Feel a slight scooping, hollowing or zipping up. Don't hold your breath or squeeze tightly. Release. Now pull up your pelvic floor muscles. Release. Breathing evenly, engage both sets of internal muscles, keeping your stomach and buttocks soft. Engage your core during everyday tasks: this gives particularly good support while driving.

317

Safe lifting

To safeguard the spine and joints in age, remember the rules of lifting and carrying: keep heavy loads close to your centre of gravity, distribute weight evenly on right and left and when picking up and putting down bend your legs, not your spine. Consciously engage your core muscles and inhale as you lift, exhale as you put down. If you have to carry heavy bags frequently, invest in a rucksack with padded shoulder straps, safer for the spine than carrying loads over one shoulder.

318

Improve your stroke

Look for a swimming stroke master class to ensure bad posture doesn't hinder efficiency in the pool. Being aware of good posture in each stroke streamlines and co-ordinates leg and arm movements, protects the back, neck and joints, and expands lung capacity. You will notice improved stamina and power in the water, too. Teachers trained in the Shaw Method, which applies the skills of the Alexander Technique to swimming, report remarkable improvements in older swimmers.

Breathing essentials

Deep breathing slows the heart rate, regulates blood pressure, dissipates muscular tension and restores mental and emotional equanimity. It also cleanses the body and makes exercising more effective.

319

Check your breathing

Rest one palm on your chest, the other on your abdomen. Close your eyes and watch what happens as you breathe normally. Which hand moves? If it is the upper hand you are breathing shallowly, restricting the flow of rejuvenating oxygen. On your next inhalation imagine the breath dropping into the bottom

Use breath rebalancing exercises to keep breathing easy and restful.

hand, bypassing your chest. Feel your belly swell with the in-breath and draw back slightly with each out-breath.

320

Rebalancing breath

Sit upright, either on a chair or cross-legged, with hands resting palm upward on your thighs, elbows and shoulders relaxed. Watch your breathing.

Placing the tips of your right thumb and fingers together, take a breath in through your nose. At the same time imagine a flow of energy moving in through your left hand and up the left side of your body.

Open your right hand and close the left hand, breathing out. Feel energy sweeping down the right side of your body and out through the hand.

Now breathe in through the right side, close the right hand, open the left hand and breathe out. Repeat, alternating hands.

321

Fill your lungs

Sit quietly with your eyes closed. Breathe into the bottom third of the lungs, then stop. Now breathe into the middle part of the lungs, widening the ribs, then stop. Finally, fill the top part of the lungs. Breathe out in a slow, controlled way, from the top down.

322
Expand your ribs

Pilates teachers encourage full use of the lungs by asking you to imagine the rib cage expanding sideways as you inhale. Place your palms on your ribs, fingers facing forward. Inhaling, feel your ribcage expand to the side. Exhaling, feel the ribs contract. Swivel your hands so your fingers lie over your back ribs. Breathing in, feel these expand, then contract as you exhale. Remove your hands and repeat, picturing the ribs widening at front and back.

323
Breathing into the back

Sit with your buttocks resting on your heels. Keeping your weight anchored in your buttocks, bend forward gradually, so that your chest rests on your thighs, forehead on the floor and arms by your sides, hands resting by your toes. Breathing in, feel your lower back and ribs expand. Notice the contraction on the out-breath. Repeat for 3 minutes.

324
Keep counting

If it helps you to focus in any of the breathing exercises, count as you breathe in and out, choosing a number, such as three or four, that you can complete easily, without gasping for breath.

Aerobic workout

Aerobic exercise that challenges the heart and lungs by using large numbers of muscle groups continually for at least 20 minutes improves the functioning of these vital organs even if you're in your 60s and have never exercised before, according to a US study into ageing.

325
Never too late

Take heart from remarkable studies showing that people aged 85 could improve their aerobic capacity by as much as 20 per cent by following a 12- to 16-week programme of exercise in which the heart rate reached more than 75 per cent of its maximum aerobic capacity. For optimum results, aim for an hour's exercise a day: women in their 70s who did so in a study at a US university demonstrated aerobic abilities of women 30 years younger.

326
Buy a pedometer

Track exactly how many steps you take per day. Guidelines suggest a minimum daily target of 5,000 steps (about 4km/2½ miles), usually achievable through incidental everyday activity. Any less and you lead a sedentary life. To move into the active category, step up to 10,000 steps or more by adding in extra

Buy a pedometer then set yourself a daily target of at least 5,000 steps.

walks before work, at lunchtime or in the evening and using stairs instead of lifts.

327
Warming up

As we age, joints lose mobility, tendons stiffen and muscles shrink. As muscle fibres decrease, they can take longer to respond to stimulus, making injury more likely. Warm up and cool down every time you exercise to reduce risk. Before exercising, spend 7–10 minutes warming large muscles and lubricating joints: shrug and roll your shoulders; circle hips, wrists and ankles. Bend and straighten your legs a few times. Then add in larger movements that raise the pulse and increase circulation to muscles. March on the spot, swinging your arms, for example.

328
Co-ordination games
Add co-ordination tasks into your warm-up, such as walking along a balance beam and raising opposite arms and legs. Write your name in space using different parts of the body – hips, shoulder, elbow – or follow imaginary paths around a room that twist and turn.

329
Think tall
Before starting a movement, think tall, engage the core muscles in your abdomen and pelvic floor and think about maintaining space between each vertebra. Move the crown of your head towards the sky and let this lift your torso. As you breathe in imagine your chest widening, like opening a book from its spine.

330
Move like a crab
Try side-to-side movements, such as sideways galloping, grapevine steps and side lunges. These are challenging for body and brain and so demand greater care and intensity (and burn more calories).

331
Working aerobically
After warming up, spend 20 minutes on more strenuous exercise. Take a power walk or jog; step up and down using a stair or fitness step (change the lead foot every minute); cycle at moderate intensity; swim laps; bounce on a mini trampoline; put on music and dance. If at any time you feel pain, faintness or are uncomfortably out of breath, ease off and start to cool down.

332
Lost in music

Listening to music while you exercise helps give you the enthusiasm to keep up the intensity for the full 20 minutes. Download appropriate tunes on your iPod: choose a lightweight version with an armband or belt clip so you don't have to carry it. Alternatively, make yourself an exercise tape or CD. Choose beats you can move in sync with – studies suggest this makes exercisers train at higher intensity – and vary the tempo for warming up, high impact work, cooling down and chilling out. During the aerobic section, take the tempo up and down rather than starting slow and getting faster.

333
Calculating intensity

For cardio work to be effective you must work at a level of intensity higher than when the body is at rest for at least 20 minutes three times a week. Aim to stay at around 60–75 per cent of your maximum heart rate. To calculate your heart rate, buy a monitor or exercise your brain by counting your pulse. Find your pulse at the side of your neck with your first two fingers. Count the beats over six seconds. Multiply by 10 to find out how many beats per minute (BPM). This is your heart rate. A typical 35 year old should keep her

When skipping, lift your knees higher as you get warmer.

heart rate during 20 minutes cardio work between 111 and 138 BPM. This drops to 102–127 BPM by age 50 and to 93–115 BPM by 65.

334
Take the talk test

If you can't talk while exercising, you're training too hard. When you're working at your hardest, count out loud to keep within an effective training zone. This is not an excuse for chatting!

335
Skipping

This is great for concentration and co-ordination, and for keeping bones strong. Alternate the leading

foot, switch to jumping with both feet and turn the rope forward and back. Look ahead, not at the floor. When you feel confident, experiment with fancy footwork. Try skipping with children to learn the coolest tricks and rhymes.

336
Challenge yourself

Being able to work out intensely may be a key to long life. One study established that people who could achieve a high level of intensity during cardiovascular exercise tended to have increased longevity when compared with exercisers who merely ambled along. Bear this in mind when you feel like giving up.

337
Interval training

Boost your capacity for aerobic exertion (and longevity) by breaking up your regular cardiovascular work with short bursts of intense activity. Vary jogging with sprinting, run on the spot in the pool, interrupt brisk walking with 30 seconds of jumping jacks or find a hill to cycle up. When walking, add in expansive skipping movements, bringing knees to hip height and exaggerating the movement forward and back of alternate arms. This augments your lung capacity and expands the chest, enabling more youthful breathing.

Working with weights

Beyond the age of 40 shrinking muscle tissue means loss of strength. Regular muscle-building exercise may slow or even reverse this decline and help maintain a more youthful metabolism suggests research in *The Journals of Gerontology*. It preserves bone mass, too.

338
How heavy?

Start with a weight you can lift comfortably 10–15 times (one set of repetitions). Make sure you can achieve the same full range of movement in the muscle with the weight as you can without. You should be able to guide the weight down in as controlled a manner as when you lift it. When, after practice, the action starts to feel easy (for example, you could lift 20 times without noticing) progress to the next level of weight. Start with 1.5kg weights and progress to 2.5kg; men can start with the higher weight and move up to 4kg.

339
How often?

Aim for three 10-minute sessions with weights every week, with a day's rest between each routine. If you stick with this you'll see results quickly – you will look toned and firm and feel fitter – which fosters motivation.

Weights workouts become more important as we age.

340
Short sessions

If you lack time for a full weights workout, don't miss out completely. A study reported in the *Journal of the American Geriatrics Society* suggested older people who completed a reduced set of strength-training exercises still improved in muscle strength and the ability to perform physical tasks – although those who did the full complement saw greater benefits.

341
Get advice

Don't start working out with free weights or on fixed-weight machines until you have completed an induction with a trainer at a gym. For your first few sessions, don't muddle through – ask a coach for advice and to help monitor your initial work.

342
Adding sets

Start with one set of repetitions (10–15 lifts of the weight), then take a break. If your muscles feel sufficiently overloaded, stop the exercise there and move onto the next movement. If not, work up to three sets of repetitions, taking a short break between each set to stretch out the muscles worked. You know best how far to push yourself.

Create your own weights: bags of rice or tins of food work well.

343
Tins and bags

Lifting and walking with heavy objects counts as weight-bearing exercise. Try using tins of food and work up to bags of potatoes. Look for weights opportunities in everyday life, too: wheelbarrow loads, tins of paint, watering cans and shopping bags.

344
Hand-held weights

With a set of dumbbells you can do weights work any time, whenever the urge strikes or you have 10 minutes free. It's essential to learn how to use them safely, monitoring your posture throughout and making sure your lower back is protected. Start practising with very light weights under the guidance of an instructor or in front of a mirror until you can feel as well as see the correct form and have gained the stamina to progress.

345
Using machines at the gym

Weights machines in gyms are great for beginners because you don't have to worry about your posture and co-ordination, your lower back is well supported and the movement is isolated in the muscle groups you plan to work. Ask an instructor to monitor your first few sessions if you feel uneasy or forget what to do.

346
Lifting with style

Fast, jerky movements with hand weights and on weights machines risk injuring muscle and connective tissue, so aim for a smooth, flowing technique, and don't forget to breathe as you work. When lifting and lowering, try counting to four or six and use the same count on the way down. As you master lifting the weight, you can reduce the count to two or three.

347
Ad breaks

Keep light hand weights or weights straps handy when watching TV. Every time there's an ad break, grab your weights, sit upright or stand and complete a set of biceps curls. Try to work opposing muscle groups during one break.

348
Using bodyweight

If you don't want to use weights, your body may provide enough resistance for a weights workout, for instance in push-ups, triceps dips on a chair and in many yoga postures. In water workouts enjoy the resistance offered by the water. You might also enjoy high impact sports, and exercises that stretch and contract muscles, such as rowing.

349
When to stop

Mild discomfort is to be expected (and enjoyed as a sign of muscles working hard) but stop weights work and take a breather, stretching out, if at any point you find it hard to catch your breath, the muscles start to burn, you feel sudden pain or you can't maintain good posture. Move down a weight size and try again or come back to the exercise when you feel stronger, perhaps in a couple of weeks' time.

Honing problem areas

Some parts of the body age more quickly than others. Exercises that target features such as a sagging butt, droopy breasts, excess skin around the stomach and upper arms will increase muscle tone – but be realistic about results.

350

Pelvic floor lift

Stave off problems such as incontinence, which are often associated with a weakened pelvic floor, with these exercises. Draw up the muscles around your vagina and anus, as if trying to stop yourself peeing. Hold for 10 seconds (breathing, and keeping the stomach, legs and buttocks soft). Rest and repeat up to 10 times. Squeeze and release quickly 10 times. Then lift the muscles in stages, as if going up in a lift. Hold at the top then relax down in stages. Repeat five times. Work for five minutes 3–10 times daily.

351

Wall press-up

To tone your chest and arms, try this. Stand a pace or so in front of a wall, legs hip-width apart, arms wider than shoulder distance apart, palms to the wall. Exhaling, bend your elbows to bring your body forward, elbows in line with shoulders, heels on the floor.

352

Bust benefits

Working the muscles around the chest and upper arms helps to keep the breasts perky. Build up over time to three sets of 12. If you find this exercise easy, place your hands further apart or point your fingertips towards each other.

1 Lie on your front. Place your palms beneath your shoulders, legs hip-width apart. Push on your hands lifting your body, to straighten your arms and come up onto your hands and knees.

2 Breathing out, draw your stomach muscles towards your lower back. Bend your elbows to take your chest nearer the floor. Look down and slightly forward to keep your spine long. Hold. Breathing in, return to the starting position.

Inhaling, push back to the starting position. Build up to three sets of 12 reps whenever you get the chance.

353
Waist whittler

Lie on your back with knees bent and hip-width apart, feet flat on the floor. Bend up your leg, so your right ankle rests on your left knee. Place your hands beside your ears and tuck in your chin slightly.

Breathing out, draw your abdominal muscles towards your lower back and lift your left arm and shoulder towards your right knee, keeping your chest broad. Don't try to lift too high.

Breathing in, return your elbow to the floor and repeat 8–12 times. Repeat on the other side. Work up to three sets on each side.

354
Top thigh toner

Lie on your front, with your brow resting on your hands, feet together, with a medium-sized ball placed between your thighs.

Breathing in, draw your tummy muscles towards your spine. Feel a hollowing beneath your stomach: imagine a strawberry is placed there and you do not want to crush it. Breathing out, squeeze your inner thighs and heels towards each other without engaging your buttocks. Hold the squeeze for one full breath in and out.

Release and repeat 8–12 times. Work up to three sets, keeping your abdominal muscles engaged throughout. Push on your palms to take your buttocks to your heels, arms stretching forward. Rest here for two minutes.

355
Best butt exercise

This exercise helps to combat sagging muscles around the buttocks and thighs. For extra work, draw the knees closer together or hold at the top of the lift for a number of full breaths in and out. Work up to three sets in total.

1 Lie on your back, knees bent and hip-width apart, feet flat on the floor, outside edges parallel, arms by your side with palms facing down. Draw your abdominal muscles towards your back throughout the movement.

2 Breathing in, engage the muscles in the buttocks and back of the thighs and raise the pelvis away from the floor. Hold at the top for one breath in and out. Roll down with the out-breath in a controlled manner. Repeat 12 times.

Arm improver: keep your back close to the chair and shoulders relaxed.

356
Absolute arm improver

Sit on the front of a chair, feet hip-width apart. Ease yourself forward and place your hands on the edge of the seat on either side of your buttocks. Support your bodyweight with straight arms (don't lock your elbows), knees bent.

Breathing out, bend your elbows to lower your torso until your shoulders are in line with them.

Breathing in, push on your hands to return smoothly to the starting position. Work up to 12 repetitions.

357
Fab ab exercise

Keeping the core muscles that support the torso in good alignment helps you retain a youthful silhouette. In this lift don't come up too high. As soon as the tummy bulges outward come down a little. Work up to 3 sets.

1 Lie on your back with knees bent and hip-width apart, feet flat on the floor. Place your hands beside your ears, relaxing the elbows on the floor, if possible. Tuck in your chin slightly to lengthen the back of your neck.

2 Breathing out, draw your abdominal muscles towards your lower back and lift your head, arms, shoulders and upper back. Hold, taking a breath in and out. Breathing in, lower your upper body back to the floor. Repeat 8–12 times.

Cooling down

At the end of an exercise session, leave enough time to cool down to bring your heart rate, breathing and temperature nearer normal (failure to do so can lead to dizziness, cramps and soreness next day). As we age, muscles lose moisture, making them stiffer. Stretching stimulates lubrication of the tissue, and stretching out muscles while warm increases their length and flexibility, reducing risk of injury and keeping the spine, pelvis and hips mobile.

358
Slowing heart rate
Bring body temperature back to normal by walking around the room for 5 minutes, gradually making your movements slower as your heart rate returns to normal. This helps return blood circulation to the organs and brain, guarding against fainting and dizziness. When you no longer feel sweaty or out of breath, move on to stretching.

359
Stretch your legs
Stand facing a wall, one foot a good step behind the other. Press into the wall, front knee bent, and feel a stretch through the back heel. Place the ball and toes of the front foot on the wall and bend that knee to stretch the lower calf. Take the same foot to its buttock and hold, knees together. Turn your back to the wall, extend the same leg forward (toes raised), bend the standing leg and pivot forward to feel stretch at the back of the thigh. Repeat on the other leg.

360
Extend your arms
Interlinking fingers, turn your palms to face front and extend your arms forward, feeling the shoulder blades open. Raise your hands overhead and hold. Release and bend your left arm. Placing your right hand below your left elbow, guide the arm backward, taking the left palm towards the shoulder blade. Repeat on the other arm. Interlink your fingers beside your buttocks and raise the arms up and back; feel the chest opening.

361
Relaxing forward
Kneel with feet together, buttocks on your heels, palms resting on your thighs. Sit tall for a few breath cycles.

Relaxing forward, inch your arms forward until you come to rest with arms fully extended.

Open your knees wide. Exhaling, hinge forward from the hips, place your hands on the floor and ease forward, leading with the crown. **Focus on your breathing** for up to three minutes, releasing tension with every exhalation. Come up slowly, head last.

362
Elongating front and back

Lie on your back with legs outstretched and arms extending behind your head. Stretch the front of the body by extending from toes to palms. Imagine touching both sides of the room. Now press through your heels and up to your fingernails, drawing your abdominal muscles towards the floor. Feel the stretch along the back of the body. Sense the difference between front and back.

363
Imagine the stretch

In a study reported in the *Journal of Sports Sciences,* people who visualized muscles elongating as they engaged in stretching exercises found flexibility came more easily. Another study found that people who imaged doing push-ups increased their push-up strength half as much as those who actually did the push-ups. As you stretch, picture the muscles you are working lengthening and becoming more dense and youthfully juicy.

Float and relax after water exercise, allowing your body and mind to let go.

364
Motivation visualization

Sit quietly after an exercise session and close your eyes. Notice how you feel: you might feel clean or as if you've grown two inches. Does your skin seem flushed with health? Do your spine or fingertips tingle with energy? Memorize the sensations. When you next doubt you have time to exercise, sit quietly, close your eyes and bring yourself back to this exquisite feeling.

365
Just float

After water exercise, relax completely by floating. Lie back, immersing the back of your head in the water, and let everything go. Widen your limbs to form a star, bring the soles of your feet together or stretch arms and legs away. Slow the inhalation to fill every part of your lungs and help you float. Let go, trusting the water and your breath.

366
Total relaxation

At the end of a session, lie on your back on a rug or mat with palms facing upward. Your face should be comfortably parallel to the floor; if it isn't, place a small cushion beneath your head. Check through your body to see if you are tense anywhere. It is usually helpful to take the legs and arms wider apart until you feel the joints and muscles release. Let go of your jaw and mouth, and feel as if your face is without expression as the skin softens. Relax your eyelids and look inside yourself. Breathe into that inner space and let any thoughts drift through your mind without catching hold of them. Rest here for 10–20 minutes.

Hand and foot mobility

Keeping your wrists and ankles mobile as the decades pass means movements of the hands and feet remain easy, and independent life becomes more likely into old age. You can perform exercises to help maintain mobility at your desk or in the car as well as in the exercise studio.

Keep hands mobile by regularly squeezing a hand exercise ball.

367
Ball squeeze
Keep a small rubber ball on your desk or beside the bed. Squeeze it in your palm for up to a minute twice a day to exercise your hands.

368
Finger mobility
Using the palm of one hand, gently press the back of the fingers of the other hand towards the inner arm and hold. Opening the palm, draw the fingers back, trying to take them towards the forearm. Repeat with the thumb. Repeat on the other hand.

369
Wrist mobilizer
Place your palms together in front of your chest, thumbs touching your sternum. Bring them down until you feel a stretch behind the wrist and can no longer keep the palms pressed together. Work to keep the finger pairs lengthening upward and the palms touching.

370
Foot reviver
Start by kneeling, then tuck the toes of your right foot under. Step forward with your left foot and gradually take your bottom towards your right heel, increasing the stretch on the back toes. Repeat on the other side. Try this for stiff, tired feet, but if you find this exercise uncomfortable, exert pressure very gently.

371
Spread your toes
Remove your shoes and socks. Look at your toes. Lift them and try to stretch each digit away from its neighbours. Aim for a gap between each toe. It can help to spread the fingers wide as you practise.

372
Stay grounded
Stand with feet parallel and hip-width apart. Spread your toes. Close your eyes if you want to. Imagine the soles of your feet sinking slightly into soft earth and growing roots. Now feel whether there is equal weight on both feet. Do you have more weight on the heels or the toes?

(For a clue look at the heels of your shoes.) Visualize your stance like a mountain, broad and strong. Breathe.

373
Pencil pick-up

With bare feet, practise trying to pick up pencils with your toes only.

374
Ankle circling

Holding a wall with your right hand, bend your left knee to lift the leg slightly. Imagine your big toe is a pen and draw a circle the size of a plate on the floor without moving the rest of your leg. Isolate the movement in the ankle joint. Work in the other direction, making the circle as wide as possible. Repeat on the other leg.

375
Golf ball roll

Roll a golf ball under your foot for two minutes. This provides the sole of the foot with a great massage and is particularly good if you have foot cramp or arch strain.

376
Tennis ball flex

To improve balance as well as flexibility in knees, ankles and toes, stand side on to a wall and place a small ball, such as a tennis ball, between your ankles. Breathing out, bend your knees and sink your hips, keeping the ball secure and heels down. Inhaling, come back to standing. On your next inhalation rise onto tiptoes, keeping the ball wedged between your ankles. Exhaling, come back to the starting position. Repeat a few times.

377
Feldenkrais arm circling

Use this exercise after work to release tension and mobilize the muscles in your shoulders and upper back. Keep your shoulders soft and heavy. When you meet areas of resistance, move extremely slowly to ease out stiffness.

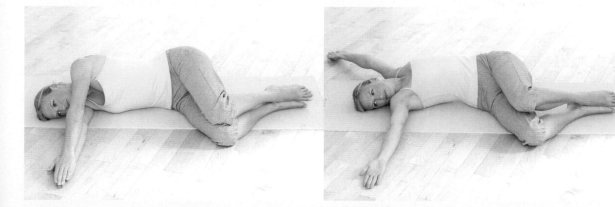

1 Lie on one side with your knees bent up easily and your arms stretched out in front of you at shoulder height, palms together. Support your head with a small cushion, if you find this more comfortable.

2 Breathing naturally, extend the top arm up over your head and around behind your back in a clockwise circle until it rejoins the other arm. Repeat in an anticlockwise direction. Roll over and repeat on the other side.

Facial exercises

Don't neglect the face in your daily exercise routine. Targeted, precise movements of the 91 facial muscles can keep face and eyes feeling youthfully energized. Ageing brings a gradual loss of tone and flexibility in the eye muscles, and signs of stress and tiredness show quickly here. Rejuvenating eye exercises to perform at your desk also demand brain-enhancing concentration.

378
Clock eye exercise
Keeping your neck long and head still, open your eyes wide and look up. Hold, then look down. Look left, hold, then right. Look to the top left, hold, then bottom right. Look top right, then bottom left. Let your eyes circle an imaginary clock face, first one way, then the other, very slowly and without moving your head.

379
Blink as you work
Eyes dry out during work at a computer screen because we lose the urge to blink. Cultivate a habit of blinking every time you check your emails. Drink plenty of water.

380
Wide gazing
Hold your index finger a little way in front of your face. Stare at the finger. Now widen your eyes so the finger blurs. Drop your finger and try to maintain the blurred wide gaze, without blinking. When it slips, replace your finger and repeat.

381
Eye cupping
Rub your palms together briskly until they tingle. Quickly cup the face and feel energy transfer to your cheeks, forehead and eye area. Don't press on your eyelids. Bring your fingers together, open your eyes and stare into the darkness of your palms without blinking while taking long, deep breaths.

382
Get an eye test
It is natural for eyes to change with age and for eyesight to deteriorate. If you notice eyesight changes – it becomes more difficult to read small type or your night vision seems reduced, for instance – book an examination with an optometrist immediately. Even if you don't have any problems with your eyesight, after the age of 40 book an appointment every one or two years to look for common age-related ailments; annually over 60.

383
Face dancing
Put on a short piece of music and dance along to it with your face only. If you can record moving images, make a film of yourself to make you laugh later. Try different pieces of music: Vivaldi works well, but mix in John Coltrane, Tammy Wynette or thrash metal, to match your mood.

384
Forehead workout
Frown and try to bring the corners of your eyebrows together. Hold, then relax. Looking forward with relaxed eyes, lift your eyebrows towards your hairline, without moving your head. Hold. Let the eyebrows go, closing your eyes and feeling your upper eyelashes weighted on your cheeks.

385
Neck lift
Roll your shoulders up, back and down to release tension. Then repeat, moving in the opposite direction.

Keeping your shoulders immobile, press your chin forward, hold for a moment, and draw back. Gently tilt your chin to point at the ceiling (avoid doing this if you have neck problems). Don't allow your head to flop backward.

Bring your back teeth together to stretch the neck. Without moving your chin, swallow seven times to stimulate the thyroid gland. This action may take some time. Gently lower the head. Tuck your chin in slightly and take it towards your chest. Hold this position for a moment, then pivot back to centre.

386
Energizing facial yoga

When your face feels tired or "set" after a period of concentration, open your eyes wide, open your mouth and stick out your tongue to touch your chin. Hold for a few seconds, roaring like a lion if it helps.

387
Combating tiredness

When your face looks and feels over-tired, heed the warning signs and use them as a prompt for you to slow down and take a break. Rearrange social plans and rethink overtime commitments. Then relax in a warm bath, apply a face pack, and place cooled damp green tea bags over your eyes. When finished, go straight to bed.

388
Mouth and cheek toning

Improve muscle tone and skin elasticity by spending just a few short minutes a day doing these exercises. Practise in front of a mirror at first to ensure that you are not screwing up your eyes.

1 Open your mouth in an "O" shape. Drop your jaw downward very slowly to make an oval. Hold, feeling the stretch in your cheeks.

2 With your teeth together, draw the sides of your mouth outward, as if saying "eee". Hold without wrinkling the skin around your eyes.

3 Pull the sides of your mouth upward into a wide smile. Hold, then pull them further up. Hold, then release. Repeat 5 times.

Building energy

Human circadian rhythms, or our internal body clock, govern different times of day, regulated by complementary drives: the urge for wakefulness and towards sleep. Energy patterns vary also according to the seasons, adapting to suit the long, dark winter nights and long, light summer days. Natural energy comes from tuning into and adapting life to fit in with shifting internal and external energy patterns.

389
Seasonal living

Occasionally try to bypass the artificial rhythms of the clock. If commitments allow, sleep late in winter, waking only when the sun rises. Let your body clock shift backward through springtime, so that by the summer you are waking and getting up and about early, again following the sun. Make the most of extra time on summer mornings by meditating and doing yoga exercises.

390
Energy scan

Close your eyes and scan your body to check your energy levels on waking and at bedtime, before work and exercise and when lying, standing and sitting. Where do you feel energy tingling and a sense of wakefulness? Notice areas of stiffness. Which areas fail to respond as you tune in? How do your fingers and toes feel? What about your neck, forehead and abdomen? Does your heart feel heavy or light? Don't judge yourself, just make a mental note of the patterns. After exercising, meditation or yoga, repeat the scan. Do you feel more connected, have areas of tension dissipated, are new parts tingling with a new vibrancy?

391
Energizing breath

Lie with your hands resting on your belly. Scan your body to check how you feel. As you breathe in, picture energy recharging an energy reservoir deep inside your abdomen. Take a minute or two to charge up this well of energy fully. On an out-breath, exhale energy from this store to your peripheries – your hands, feet and brain – and to areas of the body that feel weak, achy, dense and unresponsive. Work for 3–5 minutes. Stop and sense how recharged you feel.

392
Engage the tan tien

When exercising, walking, cycling or lifting, feel movement begin in the energy centre located in the centre of the belly. This can transform posture and energy levels. In Traditional Chinese Medicine, this area is regarded as one of the body's main wells of energy and is known as the tan tien.

393
Swap places

Most people in exercise classes choose a particular spot and stick to it week in, week out. In your next class go to the front if you usually haunt the back row, or move left or right. See what difference it makes to your energy levels and focus.

394
Reviving exercise

If you are feeling sluggish in the afternoons or after work, try a little reviving exercise by taking a swift walk or jog around the block. Expending energy in exercise helps maintain energy levels because it expands the ability of the heart to pump oxygenated blood around the body. This in turn increases your ability to process and use oxygen, an ability which declines with age, even if you are otherwise fit and healthy.

395
Capture the sun's energy
Meditate outdoors as the sun rises. Imagine the sun filling a reservoir of energy within you that will keep you going throughout the day.

396
Backward walking
When you have been concentrating on work for hours and nothing makes sense any longer, take a walk backward for a few paces. This can be enough to stun the brain into fresh responses.

397
Ear massage
Squeeze and release the ear between thumb and index finger, working from the lobe up the side and around to where the ear meets the scalp. If you find points of tension, gently apply pressure. Finally, roll the lobe between finger and thumb and give it a few swift tugs. Repeat on the other ear.

398
Hair tugs
For instant awakening, tap fingertips lightly over your scalp, from front to back. Twist handfuls of hair around index fingers and give them a light tug, working back from your forehead and temples to the nape of your neck.

399
Alertness at the wheel
Inhaling cinnamon is associated with improved alertness while driving, suggests research at a

university in West Virginia. Place 2 drops of essential oil on a handkerchief and keep handy during journeys.

400
Sealing-in energy

After yoga or meditation, lie on your back, legs wider than hip-width apart, toes dropping outward, arms away from your side, palms upward. Close your eyes and follow your breathing until you feel calm. Imagine there is a piece of chalk by your left big toe. Picture drawing a protective white outline around your body with the chalk. Work up your inner left leg very slowly, around your right leg and arm, over your head, and back down to your starting point by your left big toe. Lie in your chalk mark feeling secure in the knowledge that no energy can escape.

401
Snack on sunflower seeds

Absorb the stored energy of the sun from a handful of sunflower seeds thrown into muesli or grabbed as a snack for an anti-inertia fix. These seeds are high in B vitamins, which support adrenal function (poor functioning of these glands is associated with lack of energy).

402
Tarzan thump

Curl your fingers and lightly tap your breastbone about 5cm (2in) below your collar bones. Continue, alternating right and left hands every 20 seconds. This helps stimulate the thymus gland, which can encourage vitality.

403
Restorative shoulder massage

After a period of work at a computer screen or a long drive, re-energize your neck and shoulders with this self-massage sequence. Pay attention to areas of tightness and tension. Shake out your hands after the massage.

1 With your right hand knead down the left side of the neck, across the shoulder and down the upper arm. Repeat on the right side.

2 Making a loose fist with your right hand, pummel the top of your left shoulder and back. Repeat, bouncing your left fist over your right side.

3 Interlink fingers and cup the back of your neck. Squeeze and release from where the neck joins the head down to the top of the shoulders.

Beating fatigue

Exercise is very effective at relieving physical and mental fatigue, lifting bad moods and clearing the mind – even in old age. If, however, you find fatigue is persistent and exercise seems not to replenish but to drain you, visit a doctor to check for underlying problems, such as anaemia, depression or thyroid malfunctions.

T'ai chi promotes coordination, balance and good posture.

404
Balancing the brain

If you have trouble concentrating, speaking clearly, or get sleepy while reading or using the computer, take 6 drops of the Australian Bush Flower Essence Bush Fuschia. It is recommended to balance the left and right sides of the brain, enabling you to integrate information and communicate more fluently.

405
Cross patterning

Crossing the arms and legs is thought by kinesiologists to rebalance the right and left hemispheres of the brain, harmonizing physical and mental energies and lifting exhaustion. Stand up and circle your right arm forward, as if swimming front crawl. When the movement seems natural, co-ordinate it with a lift of your left knee. Bring both limbs high, and cross them into the opposite half of the body. Repeat with the left arm

and right leg. Finally, and most importantly, work with alternate arms and legs, as if swimming front crawl while marching on the spot.

406
Homeopathic help

At times of stress, or if your sleep has been disturbed, it helps to take regular doses (3–4 daily) of the tissue salt Kali.Phos. This restores the potassium metabolism and is a fantastic tonic for a tired nervous system. Take Arnica 30c twice a day during periods of tiredness from physical overwork or lack of sleep.

407
Bach Flower Remedies

The remedy Hornbeam is recommended for when you just can't drag yourself out of bed or into situations which require your presence. The remedy Olive is appropriate for an altogether more debilitating fatigue, which is overwhelming and the result of

overdoing things. Place 2 drops in a glass of water and sip four times a day, or as necessary.

408
Turn to t'ai chi

If you are feeling especially burnt out or fragile, turn to t'ai chi. The slow and steady flow of movements help conserve energy and work to free up blockages in the body's energy pathways, or meridians, to allow energy to flow freely again.

409
Drink water

Dehydration is a major cause of tiredness. If you find that no matter how much water you drink, you still feel fatigued and suffer from dryness of the skin, eyes, vagina and bowels, take the homeopathic remedy Nat. Mur 6c up to three times daily for a few weeks. This can stimulate your body to correct its water balance.

410
Read backwards

Read the words of this tip backwards, starting at the last line. What associations arise? If you feel tired this acts as a great pick-up.

411
Rhodiola rosea

Renowned for its anti-stress and fatigue-relieving properties, this root revives those under intense physical and mental strain. Take up to 100–200mg three times a day, with two-week breaks every three months. (Avoid if pregnant, breastfeeding or if you have bi-polar disorder.)

412
Ginseng tea

Ginseng has been used as a remedy for general weakness and debility for centuries. The root has recently been shown to have steroidal components similar to human sex hormones, which might help explain its "lifting" qualities. Drink as a tea. (Avoid if you have a medical condition or are pregnant.)

413
When to slow down

Physical symptoms of fatigue can be a sign that you need to slow down. Heed them before your body stops you by succumbing to infection.

Youthful spirit

Staying youthful in mind – by being creative, acting out of character every so often, and not taking things for granted – helps to keep the brain and body acting young, and promotes feelings of wellbeing, associated in older people with greater longevity. Fresh perspective keeps the mind resilient and adaptable, and encourages positivity, which in turn encourages immunity.

414
Do something daring

Every week do something a bit daring: run to the bottom of the garden naked, start a conversation with a stranger on a train, go skinny dipping, phone in sick, wear a shorter skirt, book a surf weekend or parachute jump, call the person you lust after and ask them out to dinner. Enjoy the new you.

415
Get creative

Try a new hobby that involves making something. Throw clay, knead dough, knit with chunky needles. Join a patchworking circle, a life-drawing class or upholstery lessons. If you prefer to be alone, sit down and start that autobiography, record your thoughts in poetry or sketch with charcoal. Studies show that being creative improves mental and physical wellbeing and memory skills, reduces depression, and leads to enhanced joie de vivre in seniors. Success breeds greater expectations of success in future endeavours.

416
Healing flowers

It's all too easy to dwell in the past when you have rather a lot of it. The Bach Flower Essence Honeysuckle helps those whose preoccupation with either "the good old days" or past traumatic events prevents full enjoyment of life in the present. Place 2 drops in a glass of water and sip four times a day or as necessary.

417
Listen to new music

Still listening to the songs of your youth? Every couple of months buy a CD by an artist you've never heard of. (Try your library and look for free downloads.) Listen to it at least five times. If you like it, follow up the back catalogue and CDs by other musicians on the recording or

Young at heart: dare to do a parachute jump to keep your spirit youthful.

label or work by the same producer. Once a year, look back at how your musical tastes have evolved.

418
Help out at playgroup
Help with a preschool group to see life afresh through the eyes of a child. Rediscover the joy of splashing colour, squidging clay, watching tadpoles grow and witnessing emotions at their most raw.

419
Give away time
Volunteer to gain fresh perspectives. In a University of Michigan study, volunteering for less than an hour a week was associated with extended life expectancy in older people – effects were most striking in those who didn't get out much.

420
Think the impossible
What did your face look like before your parents met? This is an example of a Zen koan, an unfathomable mental question which has no answer and is pondered silently as a form of meditation. By considering apparent paradoxes, you bypass the intellect and received knowledge and open your mind to all possibilities, freeing it to jump off at tangents, think intuitively, and enjoy the refreshment of new perspectives. Ponder the mysteries of your own religious tradition, such as Christ's miracles or the Sufi stories of Mullah Nasruddin.

421
Write your obituary
Write your obituary as it would read if you died tomorrow. Are you satisfied with your life? Rewrite it to reflect the life you thought you'd have when you were aged 12 or 21. Compare the two. What changes can you make to turn your current life into your wished-for life? Make practical plans to learn how to play an instrument or a new language, dance flamenco or climb Snowdon.

3 Natural beauty

What causes the skin to age prematurely? Free radical molecules in the body (due to smoking, binge drinking, bad nutrition, environmental stressors and exposure to sun) are responsible for everything from wrinkles to age spots and freckles. In this chapter you will find free-radical-busting beauty tips and treatments based on antioxidant fruit, vegetables and oils. Here, too, are recommendations for the few over-the-counter products that can transform mature skin without using chemicals that cause concern. You will also find massage treatments, yoga postures, meditation techniques, styling and haircare advice that, when put into practice, restore your youthful appearance without you having to go near a surgeon's scalpel.

Anti-ageing skin basics

From our 30s onwards, age starts to take its toll on our skin. Colour and texture become less vibrant, wrinkles and sagging start to occur, pores enlarge, capillaries break around the cheek and nose and from our 40s age spots appear on hands and cheeks, forehead and upper lip, thanks to sun exposure, pregnancy and the Pill. However, there is plenty we can do to help our skin maintain the glow of youth into our 40s, 50s and beyond.

422
Take a deep breath
Promoting oxygen flow to the skin results in visibly better tone. Learn how to breathe deeply at yoga class (see Nos. 227–29). To maximize the effects, dine on antioxidant foods such as broccoli, spinach, plums, kale and blackberries, which have a high oxygen radical absorbency capacity (ORAC).

423
Skin-saving vitamins
Build your diet around vitamin-packed fruit and vegetables. Vitamins A, C and E are strongly antioxidant and lack of vitamin A shows in flaking skin. Vitamin C is anti-inflammatory and so is essential for healing, skin cell regeneration and plumping. It works best with immune-stimulating vitamin E, which encourages circulation to promote radiance. One study showed that when taken together vitamins C and E provide double the protection from UV rays and reduce intensity of sunburn. When you check food labels vitamin C may also be listed as ascorbic acid or L-ascorbic acid, and vitamin E as alphatocopherol or tocopherol.

424
Hydrate from within
Dry skin makes wrinkles more obvious. The only natural relief from dry skin is ample hydration. Drink 2 litres (3½ pints) of water daily to plump up skin, give hair gloss, flush out toxins and help relieve headaches that can lead to frown lines.

425
Healing exercise
Older people who exercise regularly seem to have skin that heals more speedily when compared with the skin of sedentary people. Set yourself the target of 30 minutes activity most days (see No 207).

426
Moisturize while damp
Apply moisturizer and body oils to still damp skin immediately after showering or bathing. This seals in moisture and acts as a barrier to drying environmental conditions, such as wind and air conditioning.

427
Necessary fats
Research suggests that people with prematurely aged skin are deficient in essential fats, which moisturize skin from the inside, reduce inflammation and enhance mood. Fill up on oily fish, such as mackerel and sardines, linseed (flaxseed), hemp and olive oil, avocados, nuts and seeds. For maximum absorption, make nut, seed and fruit oils the fats you choose for massage oils, body lotions and intensive moisture treatments, too.

428
Destress your skin
Stress can bring on breakouts of spots, a pallid complexion, puffy eyes and etched-in frown lines. Nourish yourself with good food through stressful periods and by taking regular exercise. Try to

incorporate a weekly yoga class into a busy schedule. If city pollutants stress your skin, build more protective antioxidant fruit and vegetables into your diet and use free-radical busting grapeseed oil and green tea on the skin.

429
Stop smoking

Smoking is the second most effective way to age skin after sun exposure. Research suggests the skin of smokers over 30 ages twice as fast as the skin of non-smokers. Indeed, "smoker's skin" is a diagnostic term used to denote a grey complexion, wrinkles, dilated pores and failure to heal. Smoking constricts blood vessels, reducing oxygen and nutrient flow, produces a collagen-destroying enzyme and creates wrinkles as lips purse to inhale and eyes squint through smoke. Stop smoking (see Nos. 688–706).

430
Prioritize beauty sleep

Sleep is necessary for regeneration and cell restoration. During sleeping hours growth hormones responsible for renewing and restoring skin, hair and bones are secreted. Sleep loss shows first beneath the eyes and in a dulled complexion. To enhance sleep see Nos. 802–26.

431
Age-relate your beauty regime

Look for age-specific skincare products targeted at the skin and lifestyle demands of your own age group. The anti-ageing requirements of 30-something skin, for example, differ from those of post-menopausal skin. Natural beauty company Yin Yang recommends its pH-Amino 4 Cream for use after the menopause – its plant protein and wheatgerm oil formulation promotes skin healing and regeneration.

Boost absorption of necessary fats by using body lotions based on nut, seed and fruit oils.

Skincare in the sun

There's no escaping the fact that UV rays lead to premature skin ageing, but research reveals that it also enhances mood, protects bone density, and may even safeguard against cancer thanks to vitamin D, which is created by the skin during sun exposure.

432

Safer sunblocks?

Some natural healthcare specialists worry about the negative effects of repeatedly applying sunscreens containing chemical UV-light "sponges" over large areas of skin. These oestrogen-mimicking chemicals have been detected in urine and breastmilk after application. Check for and avoid sun creams and make-up which contain the following ingredients: benzophone and azobenzone, PABA (para-aminobenzoic acid) and PABA esters, cinnamates and nanoparticles of titanium dioxide and zinc oxide.

433

Great natural sunscreens

Choose from reputable natural brands that don't use chemical sun filters, relying instead on the light-reflecting mineral blocks that tint the skin slightly. These include

434

Sun-protection smoothie

All the fruits in this smoothie are fantastic antioxidants and the pomegranate juice also helps protect the skin from damage caused by the sun.

- ½ mango
- ½ papaya
- slice of honeydew melon
- 1 nectarine
- 3 apricots
- 12 black grapes
- small glass of pomegranate juice

1 Slice the soft fruit away from the stones, chop up the remaining fruit and deseed the grapes, if necessary. Place all the fruit into a blender and whizz them until they are well combined.

2 Pour the smoothie into a glass and top up with chilled pomegranate juice, stirring well to combine. Drink immediately. Pomegranate juice has been shown to extend the SPF of a sunscreen by as much as 20 per cent.

Dr Hauschka, Green People, Weleda, Origins Beach Blanket and Neal's Yard Remedies.

435
Soak up some sun

Exposing non-sunblocked skin to the sun for 5–15 minutes three times a week supplies a healthy dose of vitamin D. Do this especially during winter months if you have dark skin and live in the northern hemisphere.

436
Keep your hat on

Prevent age-related pigmentation problems worsening over time by wearing a wide-brimmed dark hat in the sun. Uncover only before 11am and after 4pm, when rays are less intense. Cover up, too, your décolletage, an area of skin that crinkles with sun exposure.

437
After-sun bath

If your skin feels sore after sunning, apply soothing cider vinegar on cotton-wool swabs or pour a cup into tepid bathwater.

438
Avoid sunbeds

UV rays from sunbeds may cause the breakdown of folic acid in the body – this B vitamin seems to protect against some later-life diseases, such as dementia and cardiovascular disease. Using sunbeds may also worsen age-related pigmentation problems.

439
Faking it

Fake tan and tanning moisturizers have been associated with DNA damage because of their active ingredient dihydroxyacetone (DHA). Look for organic self-tanners, such as Green People's Organic Self-Tan Lotion, which contains no heavy metals.

440
Sun-repair snacks

Eat orange and dark green foods for their beta-carotene, lutein and zeaxanthin content, which can protect against sun damage. Foods rich in vitamin E, such as green leafy vegetables, help reduce redness caused by sun exposure.

Eternal style

Women over the age of 40 now make up more than 50 per cent of the UK female population. Some retailers regard us as the future of fashion, since we have a well-developed awareness of trends and what flatters us and may have income to spare. But it can become increasingly difficult to fling on garments and look effortlessly chic.

441
Dress your age

There are defining moments in life when it's time to take stock of your wardrobe. Once every five years, take a hard look at staple garments, shoes and boots, underwear and swimwear, jackets and going-out outfits. Ask what they say about you. Are you reliving your 20s in your party wear and your wedding night in your underwear? Do dog-walking clothes serve for dates too? Now's the time to reinvent yourself to flatter your current age and lifestyle.

442
Seasonal dressing

To keep your wardrobe updated, buy the catwalk edition of fashion magazines each season to see what's in and what's not. Not everything you see will necessarily be easy or practical to wear. Look at how

perennial labels, such as Chanel and Armani, make slight changes to freshen up a look; see what collections designed by older women, such as Chloe, Donna Karan and Marni, have to offer.

444

Get styling advice

Book an appointment with a personal shopper at a department store or a fashion adviser at a high-street chain. They will pick out garments that fit, flatter and update your look with no obligation to buy.

445

Timeless classics

Try clean shapes and simple silhouettes, and invest in a few timeless pieces: a classic trench coat and wrap dress, a fabulous bag, great shoes. Wear stunning jewellery if you feel underdressed in classic chic. Conceal trouble spots with garments that cover the arms, are tailored to flatter a shortened torso, or offer the benefit of a plunging neckline without views of crêpey wrinkles.

443

Play to your assets

Don't cover up in oversized garments. Clothes that fit flatter. Make the most of your best bits: highlight great legs or well-turned ankles in flirty skirts and fabulous shoes; show off a long neck with a bobbed haircut.

446

Pick your palette

In daylight, stand in front of a mirror and hold your favourite garments to your face. Do the colours still suit you? If hair and skin have faded a little, you might need to adapt your palette. Rich tones might suit better than washed-out pastels; chocolate or charcoal can be kinder than black; green tones play down flushed cheeks; and creamy tones near the face reflect illuminating light upward.

447
Flower remedy
Before doing a wardrobe clearout, take 6 drops of the Australian Bush Flower Essence Five Corners – this is a great remedy for low self-esteem, especially concerning physical appearance. Tune into your sense of self-worth.

448
Detox your wardrobe
If your wardrobe makes every morning a misery, it's time to detox. Cast away anything that makes you feel fat, items that remind you of failed relationships and impulse buys with labels still attached. Create a wardrobe containing only clothes you love (and which fit and flatter).

449
What not to wear
Full-on fashion "looks" worn head-to-toe, rock-chick chic and sleeveless vests might not be appropriate to those of us who haven't maintained the training

Clothes to avoid: think about which looks create the right impression.

regime of Madonna as we enter our late 40s. Here are some other items that should now be donated to daughters or nieces:
- leather trousers
- miniskirts
- hot pants
- ra-ra and puffball skirts
- baseball caps
- the punk look
- military chic
- day-glo colours
- midriff-exposing tops
- slogan T-shirts
- animal prints

450
Ditch and switch
Get together with a bunch of girlfriends to dump and swap clothes that no longer fit or suit you. Everyone empties bags of cast-offs

into the centre of a room, then scrabbles to find a new outfit that does suit. If more than one person hankers after the same piece, you all try it on and ask for honest (but kind) opinions about what really suits you at this stage of life.

451
Burn your bra
Japanese studies suggest that the body works harder to keep breasts perky against gravity when we go bra-less. However, a well-fitting bra can offer a psychological lift. Get measured by a professional.

452
Choosing role models
When you despair of the bright young things adorning TV and magazines, look out for the models hitting 50 and beyond who are becoming the new faces of cosmetic conglomerates and fashion houses: Twiggy, Christie Brinkley, Sharon Stone and Catherine Deneuve.

453
Natural moth protection
Launder or dry clean, then store away the previous season's clothes (moths like sweat). Add cedar balls as a deterrent. If moths make inroads, place clothes in a freezer (in bags) for three weeks or zap in the microwave to kill live moths and eggs.

Organic beauty

On average, women apply some 200 chemicals to their skin each day. Yet 99 per cent of high-street skincare products contain preservatives shown to have gender-bending effects on mammals; while other chemicals used are known carcinogens or can have neurological effects. Items branded as anti-ageing are not usually the most natural choice. Green up your make-up bag and beauty routines to avoid suspect items.

454
EU safety net

Choose beauty products from the European Union, which bans the use of ingredients proven to be carcinogenic or which adversely affect the reproductive system. German products adhere to particularly stringent guidelines. The US Department of Agriculture, on the other hand, no longer certifies finished cosmetic products as organic, which may lead to increased numbers of unsubstantiated claims to organic status.

455
Check the certification

It's not enough to choose products branded "natural" to be sure they are free from potentially harmful ingredients. Without the stamp of a reputable organic accreditation body, an "organic" product might contain as little as one per cent organic matter. The cosmetic industry's trade journal points out that plants not grown organically may be contaminated with pesticides, fertilizers or bacteria. Reassuring logos include:
- The Soil Association (UK)
- BDIH (Germany)
- Demeter (international biodynamic accreditation)
- Ecocert (France)
- NASSA (Australia)
- CAQ (Quebec)

456
Steer clear of the high street

Danish research suggests that 99 per cent of "leave-on" and 77 per cent of "rinse-off" high-street beauty products contain hormone-disrupting parabens, shown to be capable of penetrating the body and reaching breast tissue. A Swedish study found reproductive-toxicant phthalates in 80 per cent of beauty products. The only way to avoid them is to shop for beauty products in whole food stores, online and in high-end boutiques that specialize in organic, or "clean", brands.

457
Moon nurtured

Some of the most reputable and effective organic skincare products are the result of biodynamic farming: growing and harvesting by the cycles of the moon and with respect for nature, ethical morals, community values and workers' wellbeing. This is as good as holistic agriculture gets: it aims to strengthen the soil and spiritual understanding for future generations, and preaches the preservation of local cultures and traditional ways. Look for the Weleda, Dr Hauschka, WALA and Primavera brands.

458
Detox the bathroom cabinet

First ditch anything in an aerosol, which pumps unhealthy solvents into the respiratory system. Then dump items packaged in plastic: unstable gender-bending chemicals in the plastic mix may leach into oily products. Favour glass bottles instead. Get rid of talc: studies link frequent genital dusting with a raised risk of ovarian cancer.

459

Rinse off toxins

Over decades of daily use you risk absorbing a cocktail of chemicals into your skin when they are smoothed over large areas of skin without rinsing off afterwards. If you opt for only a few beauty products, prioritize organic moisturizers, body lotions and sunscreens.

460

Hidden horrors

Labels on cosmetics and beauty products are notoriously difficult to decipher, requiring knowledge of Latin and biochemistry. And not everything has to be listed on the pack: fragrance ingredients (where some of the more dubious chemicals are hidden) don't have to be specified. To cut through the blurb, choose only certified organic brands.

461

Top 10 ingredients to avoid

Some ingredients are more undesirable than others – try to avoid the following:
- Petroleum-based substances – these are drying for the skin and polluting for the atmosphere.
- SLS (sodium lauryl sulphate) – this is a harsh detergent that can cause skin and eye irritation and exacerbate dry skin.

- Parfum/fragrance – this is a catch-all term for around 100 synthetic ingredients thought to trigger one third of cosmetic allergies; they don't have to appear on the label.
- Phthalates – these hormone-disrupting substances were detected by the US Centers for Disease Control and Prevention in the body of every person tested.
- Formaldehyde – this irritates the skin and is cancer-inducing.
- Parabens – these oestrogen-mimicking preservatives are found in almost all high-street cosmetics; they are known to accumulate in the body.
- DEA-, MEA-, TEA prefixes – these can irritate scalp and eyes; they may also react with impurities and preservatives to create carcinogenic substances.
- PEG – these can irritate the scalp.

462

Choosing lipstick

Make organic lipstick high on your must-have list. Because most lipsticks are packed full of preservatives to prevent infection near the mouth, each of us consumes an average 2.5kg (5½lb) in a lifetime. Skin on the lips is thinner and more sensitive to damage than other parts of the body, and so more vulnerable to up-take of toxins.

Certified organic products are expensive but are worth every penny.

Superstar ingredients

Many of the youth-enhancing nutrients, herbs and oils that play a major role in off-the-shelf natural beauty preparations are already in your vegetable rack, refrigerator or store cupboard, making it easy to create effective (and cost-effective) anti-ageing treatments at home.

463
Your anti-ageing oil kit

These essential oils are for use diluted in a base or carrier oil for massage (see No. 611), baths and conditioning treatments.

- Frankincense is great for toning, lifting and anti-wrinkle effects. It also helps to deepen breathing and enhance meditation.
- Lavender helps promote new cell growth.
- Camomile soothes dry, sensitive skin and helps reduce puffiness and broken capillaries; it also promotes elasticity and strength.
- Cypress combats puffiness caused by fluid retention.
- Neroli is good for broken veins, skin regeneration and elasticity.
- Sandalwood soothes itchy skin and rebalances mature skins.

464
Invest in the best

Although costly, essential oil of rose is one of the most effective oils for soothing thinning, sensitive skin,

Some essential oils are renowned for their anti-ageing properties.

especially after the menopause. Rose oil also affects the emotions – aromatherapists value it for lifting mood, releasing nervous tension and making a woman feel more positively feminine. Beware cheaper brands, which may be adulterated.

465
Intensive-care oil

Quick-penetrating rosehip oil is rich in omega fatty acids that promote skin elasticity and resilience. It is renowned for rejuvenating and repairing prematurely aged, sun-damaged, inflamed or scarred skin.

466
Mummify yourself

Essential oil of myrrh has a long history of use as a skin preservative, being popular in mummification! It is used by aromatherapists to prevent tissue degeneration and tone the immune system. It helps lift feelings of weakness and is cooling for those who are over-heating physically or emotionally. Burn in a room vaporizer and mix into bath and massage oils.

467
Enjoy the vine

A glass of red wine is naturally anti-ageing, but so too are grapes and oil extracted from their seeds and stems. These are rich in vitamins A, B, C and E, potent antioxidant reservatol and wound-healing OPCs (oligo proanthocyanadins) – natural anti-ageing superstars, more protectively antioxidant than vitamins A, C or E.

468
Combating city stress

Look for off-the-shelf skincare products containing extracts of the herb rhodiola if your skin is exposed to polluted cities or endures long and stressful working hours that can kickstart premature ageing. This herb enhances the body's ability to perform well during periods of physical exhaustion and recover from the negative effects of environmental stressors.

469
Grate carrots

Research suggests the constituents of carrots – beta-carotene, lutein and lycopene – could reduce intensity of sunburn. Look for off-the-shelf products containing carrot seed oil to stimulate skin cell

Carrot seed oil may reduce age spots.

renewal and protect against free-radical damage. Aromatherapists rate this oil for its ability to reduce age spots and wrinkles and for toning while promoting elasticity.

470
Topical green tea

When green tea is applied topically after sun exposure, research has shown that it reduces the degree of sunburn as well as the extent of DNA damage. It also protects from the ageing effects of exposure to environmental toxins. Use a cooled cup of green tea as a toner, to mix clay masks or to throw into the bath.

471
White tea wonder

Richer even than green tea in antioxidants is white tea. Research suggests it can prevent oxidative cell damage that causes wrinkles and reduces immunity. Look for it especially in leave-on products applied over large areas of the body.

472
Track down honey

Packed with antioxidants, honey makes a gently effective cleanser that preserves the skin's natural oils. Its humectant properties (drawing moisture to the skin) suit it to masks, too. For skin healing look

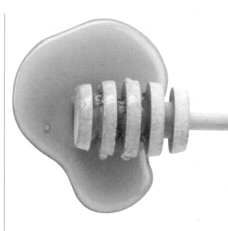

Honey is one of the most versatile of home ingredients.

for manuka honey. Living Nature's manuka honey-based products especially suit mature skin. Or try preparations based on royal jelly. Fed to the queen bee and thought to be the reason she lives 40 times longer than the worker bees, this is one of nature's most nutritive materials, containing no fewer than eight amino acids and nine vitamins. Try Burt's Beeswax and Royal Jelly Eye Creme.

473
Sea cures

Thalassotherapy centres expound the benefits of bathing in body-temperature sea water for maximum uptake of marine nutrients, and use unrefined salt crystals or sea salt mixed with antioxidant seaweed for body wraps. At home, sea salt suits gentle skin buffing (ideal for mature skin), since it dissolves when it meets warm water.

Daily facial care

Skin tone and texture often alter during and after the menopause – you might notice an unfamiliar tightness, red patches and other signs of sensitivity. A careful daily facial care routine can minimize the effects of hormone changes.

474
Cleanse before bed

Be vigilant about cleansing skin of make-up and grime before bed. Tiny traces can irritate eyes, and lead to blocked pores and dull complexion.

475
Maintain a light touch

Never pull or drag mature skin when applying cleanser. Rather, cover your fingers in the cream or oil, lay your hands over your face, press gently, then lift your fingers away one by one, in a rolling action. Repeat to cover the face and neck.

476
Make-up remover

Use this homemade remover to clean your face gently.

2 tbsp sweet almond oil
3 drops essential oil of neroli

Pour the almond oil into a clean dark glass bottle, drop in the essential oil. Lid and store in a cool, dark place. Shake before use.

477
Warm cloths

While removing make-up, place a piece of muslin to soak in a basin of warm water. Wring out and place over the face (do not rub), allowing the warmth to open the pores. Then cleanse. Repeat with cold water to close pores afterwards.

478
Milk tonic

Soak a cotton wool pad in full-fat milk. Press lightly onto the face, lifting away dirt. This also removes dead cells, encouraging cell renewal.

479
City cleanser

For city grime, replace detergents with an oil-rich, antioxidant cleanser.

1 green tea bag
1 tsp ground almonds
1 tsp grapeseed oil
1 tsp milk powder

Place the tea bag in a mug and pour over boiled water. Leave to steep.

Blend together the almond powder, oil and milk powder. Mix in enough green tea to make a smooth, cool paste. Massage over face and neck, then lift away with a warm wet face cloth. Splash with cool water.

480
For sensitive types

Sensitive skin requires particularly gentle cleansing. Try this blend.

1 tsp fine oatmeal
1 tsp jojoba oil
1 tsp milk powder
1–2 tbsp rosewater

Mix together the oatmeal, jojoba and milk powder. Stir in enough rosewater to form a smooth paste. Massage over face and neck, then lift away with a warm wet face cloth. Splash with tepid water.

481
Honey for dry skin

Secure hair away from the face. Gently massage into damp skin a good amount of honey. Rinse with plenty of tepid water, then pat dry.

482
Kitchen cupboard toners

Opt for toners rich in antioxidants: rosewater, grape juice and green tea will do nicely. Cider vinegar in cooled peppermint or fennel tea is a great pore-reducing toner.

483
Creamy cleanser

Oil-based cleansers suit ageing skin better than drying detergents.

1 tsp fine oatmeal
1 tsp avocado oil
1 tsp milk powder
½ tsp runny honey
1–2 tbsp single cream

Mix together the oatmeal, oil and milk powder. Stir in the honey and enough of the cream to make a thick paste. Smooth over the face and neck. Lift away with a warm wet face cloth. Rinse the cloth and repeat. Splash with tepid water.

484
Remember your neck

When applying moisturizer, don't forget your neck and the thin skin of your décolletage to help stave off tell-tale crêpiness and crinkling.

485
Calming influence

This moisturizer is great if your skin is irritated or sensitive.

1 green tea bag
3 drops essential oil of rosemary

2 drops essential oil of camomile
2 tbsp aloe vera gel

Place the tea bag in a mug and pour over boiled water. Leave to steep. Drop the essential oils into the aloe gel and stir well. Once the tea is cool, mix a little into the gel. Massage into cleansed skin. (Omit rosemary oil if you have epilepsy.)

486
Intense moisturizer

Blend intensely moisturizing oils for dehydrated skin.

2 tbsp hemp oil
1 tsp wheatgerm oil
1 capsule evening primrose oil
3 drops essential oil of frankincense
2 drops essential oil of neroli

Pour the oils into a clean, dark glass bottle. Prick the capsule and squeeze in the oil. Drop in the essential oils. Lid and store in a dark, cool place. Shake before use.

487
Delicate touch

This moisturizer is particularly good for thinning or delicate skin.

488
Cool as a cucumber

This cooling cucumber toning mask freshens the face and is especially effective when you feel overheated or anticipate a break out.

- 1 organic cucumber
- 1 tbsp witch hazel

1 Mixing the ingredients: roughly chop the cucumber into small chunks, place in a blender and blitz to form a rough paste. Stir in the witch hazel tincture and transfer the mixture into a bowl ready for application.

2 Apply like a mask, and relax for 5–10 minutes. You may prefer to lie down, placing cucumber slices or cooled green tea bags over your eyes. Wipe the mask away with a damp face cloth and splash with cool water.

2 tbsp apricot kernel oil
1 capsule evening primrose oil
3 drops each essential oils of
   sandalwood and neroli

Pour the apricot oil into a clean dark glass bottle. Prick the capsule and squeeze in. Drop in the essential oils. Lid and store in a dark, cool place. Shake before use.

489
Sun soother

Sun-damaged skin benefits from this regenerating moisturizer.

1 tbsp grapeseed oil
2 tsp rosehip oil
1 tsp wheatgerm oil
3 drops essential oil of lavender
1 drop each essential oils of
   camomile and geranium

Pour the oils into a clean dark glass bottle. Drop in the essential oils. Lid and store in a dark, cool place. Shake before use.

490
Off-the-shelf moisturizers

Dr Hauschka's iconic Rose Day Cream has a nurturing fragrance and helps repair weakened capillaries. REN's Phytostimuline Instant Replenishment Moisturizer plumps and addresses moisture-retention issues. Primavera's Demeter-certified Hydrating Face Cream is packed with antioxidants, essential fatty acids and anti-ageing plant oils.

Deep cleansing

Once a week, treat tired or grey-looking skin to a gentle but deep-cleansing mask or steam treatment. This lifts away dead cells and encourages the natural process of regeneration, resulting in a fresher complexion.

491
Applying masks

When smearing on facial clays and masks, don't forget to cover the neck and décolletage area, too. Lie down to relax while the mask dries. Finish with a wipe of toner and a thin layer of moisturizer.

492
Rose-scented rinse

To lift away scrubs and masks without rubbing, fill a basin with warm water. Add two drops essential oil of rose mixed into ½tsp sweet almond oil. Soak a face cloth in the water and place over the face.

493
Nourishing cream mask

Replace extreme exfoliation with this moisturizing treatment.

1 avocado
1 tbsp double cream
1–2 tbsp extra virgin olive oil

Mash the avocado. Mix in the cream and enough of the oil to make a

textured paste. Smear over cleansed skin, then lie down for 15 minutes. Lift away with a warm, wet face cloth, then splash with tepid water.

494
Dull skin clarifier

Give dull skin a lift with this clarifying face mask.

2 tsp fine oatmeal
2 tsp milk powder
½ tsp avocado oil
1 tbsp rosewater

Mix together the oatmeal and milk powder, then stir in the oil. Thin with rosewater to create a smooth paste. After cleansing, massage the paste gently into your face. Lift away with a warm, wet face cloth, then splash with cool water.

Choose honey and oats for city cleansing.

495
City know-how

The antioxidant properties of this mask make it great for city dwellers.

2 tbsp green clay
1 tsp honey
1 tsp rolled oats
1 tsp grapeseed oil
1 white tea bag

Mix the clay, honey, oats and oil. Stir in cooled tea. Smear the paste over cleansed skin. Relax for 15 minutes. Lift away with a warm, wet face cloth, then splash with tepid water.

496
Sensitive skin mask

Use this mask once a week if you have sensitive skin.

12 black grapes (with seeds)
2 tbsp runny honey
1 tsp baby rice
½ tsp (colourless) sesame oil
2 drops essential oil of rose

Whizz up the grapes in a blender then mix in the other ingredients well. Apply to cleansed skin. Relax for 15 minutes while the mask dries. Lift away with a warm, wet face cloth, then splash with tepid water.

497
Restoration and repair

Rejuvenate damaged skin with a paste made from a mashed banana mixed with 1 tbsp each double cream and runny honey. Circle onto cleansed skin. Lift away with a warm, wet face cloth, then splash with cool water.

498
Steam cleansing

Add 5 drops essential oil of sandalwood to a bowl of hot water. Cover your head and the bowl with a towel for five minutes. Inhale the aromatic steam, keeping mouth and eyes closed. (Avoid if you have asthma or a respiratory condition.)

Organic nightcare

Skin enters a renewal and repair phase at night. Under 30s probably don't need a separate night cream, but many natural skincare gurus teach that skin in later life responds well to intensive replenishing at night.

499
Applying night-cream

Don't slather face and neck with nightcare products: use only as much as can be absorbed readily by the skin. Blot away any excess with a tissue after two minutes.

500
Off-the-shelf creams

Weleda's Wild Rose Night Cream combines organic rosehip oil and evening primrose oil for their essential fatty acids with extracts of horsetail and myrrh to support skin repair. Decleor's creamy Baume de Nuit Iris contains anti-ageing carrot oil and antioxidant essential oils of geranium and camomile. Combine with Aromessence™ Iris, a blend of essential oil concentrates, for re-sculpting results.

501
Night-care oil

If you like to use a night product, why not try this oil blend.

2 tbsp sweet almond oil
1 tsp each avocado and wheatgerm oil
1 capsule evening primrose oil
4 drops essential oil of lavender
2 drops each essential oils of myrrh
  and frankincense
1 drop each essential oils of cypress

Pour the oils into a clean dark glass bottle. Drop in the essential oils. Lid and store in a dark, cool place. Shake before use. To apply, massage into cleansed damp skin.

502
Let your skin breathe

Aestheticians from the Dr Hauschka natural skincare range believe skin needs to breathe at night, and must be weaned from an addiction to rich night creams. Give the theory a try by moisturizing only in the morning; allow a few weeks for skin to settle into this more natural rhythm.

503
Massage your feet

To ensure deep sleep and relaxation that shows on the face next morning, massage your feet with warmed (colourless) sesame oil before bed.

504
Bathtime massage

A steamy bath primes skin to absorb oils and herbal extracts applied topically, making this a good time for facial massage with nourishing oils.

505
Give yourself a quick facial

Pour a little grapeseed oil or oil blend onto the palm of one hand. Rub the palms together, then rub the backs of the hands. Begin by stroking the backs of your fingers up from neck to jaw, alternating hands. Work on both sides of the neck. Repeat from jaw to cheekbone on both sides. Now run alternate index fingers from eyebrow to hair line. Circle your temples with your middle fingers, then massage the lobes of the ears, circling them between fingers and thumbs.

Facial massage can help the complexion appear smoother, firmer and more radiant.

Special care

Lots of natural products have been created to help conquer particular beauty gripes of mature skin. These include topical treatments to help minimize crêpey texture and thread veins; facial spritzers to mist the flushed and overheating; and zit zappers to tackle acne breakouts.

506
Off-the-shelf intensive care

Jurlique's phyto-nutrient-rich Wrinkle Softener is popular in Australia to combat the effects of intense sun exposure. Burt's Bees Repair Serum is a concentrated elixir of renewing oils, vitamins and herbs, and claims to be one of the most beneficial products for ageing skin on the market. The Organic Pharmacy's Antioxidant Gel and Serum is said by many users to improve the tone, colour and texture of mature skin so dramatically it's likened to an instant face-lift. Primavera's Natural Balance Ultra Rich Seed Oil Capsules are recommended to "neutralize" mature skin that is new to natural products.

507
Anti-wrinkle oil

Massage this homemade anti-wrinkle oil into cleansed skin for a rejuvenating effect.

2 tbsp hemp oil
1 tsp wheatgerm oil
1 capsule evening primrose oil
4 drops each essential oils of
   frankincense and sandalwood

Pour the oils into a clean dark glass bottle. Drop in the essential oils. Lid and store in a dark, cool place. Shake before use.

Marigolds are rich in carotenoids and flavonoids, which help strengthen veins.

508
Neck treatment oil

Sandalwood is traditional in Indian oil blends to guard against crêpey skin on the neck and chest. Mix 3 drops essential oil of sandalwood into 1 tbsp grapeseed oil and massage daily into the neck.

509
Vein treatment oil

To treat broken capillaries on the face or legs, mix together 1 tsp peach kernel oil and one drop each of essential oils of rose and camomile. Gently massage the affected area using the ring fingers. Blot excess oil with a tissue.

510
Floral vein toner

Place one camomile teabag and one marigold teabag in a mug, pour over boiling water and leave to steep for 10 minutes. Soak a cotton ball in the brew and, when cool, wipe over affected areas as a substitute for toner.

511
Herbal vein help

Witch hazel cream (also sold as Hammamelis cream) can reduce the appearance of tiny broken veins, if used regularly. Dab on to tighten and promote healing.

512
Protect your skin

In winter wrap up in a hat, scarf and turned-up coat collar to shield delicate skin from harsh winds and cold temperatures. Shun very hot water on cold mornings. Look for products rich in nut and seed oils and containing warming natural ingredients, such as ginger, black pepper and eucalyptus. Avoid overuse of alcohol as this dilates fine blood vessels and can be responsible for broken veins.

513
Concealer trick

Apply a tiny amount of concealer on a brush to disguise broken capillaries, pressing onto the surface rather than brushing.

514
Blemish blitzes

To speed the healing of blemishes, dab on cider vinegar, manuka honey or neat tea tree oil on a cotton wool ball. To calm down an inflamed spot, apply an ice cube.

515
Night treatment

Before going to bed, cover pimples with a little natural yogurt or a clay mask for its drawing action. Rinse away the remnants next morning.

Carry a cooling facial spritzer in your handbag ready to refresh a flushed face.

516
Angry red marks

Reduce the aftermath of hormonal pimples by mixing 1 drop of rosehip oil into 1 tsp of grapeseed oil. Dab this onto the affected area with a cotton ball.

517
Checking excessive perspiration

Try natural antiperspirants rather than conventional products: experiment with deodorant stones or crystals, or simply dust your skin with bicarbonate of soda or cornstarch. These may not be as effective as you are used to, so carry pump-action sprays in your bag for refreshing top-ups.

518
Cooling facial spritzer

Fill a clean pump-action spray bottle with cooled green tea. Refrigerate until required then use to refresh a flushed face. The anti-inflammatory and anti-irritant properties of green tea are good for attacks of sensitivity and itchiness, too.

519
Zapping zits with off-the-shelf products

The Organic Pharmacy's Blemish Gel comprises a blend of antiseptic herbs and essential oils. Burt's Bees Healthy Treatment Blemish Stick contains 10 herbal ingredients to correct imbalances that cause breakouts of spots.

Instant radiance

The way you react to life's stresses, be it with anger, resignation or bitterness, can become etched into your face over time. Facial muscles "set" with recurrent expressions, fixing visible lines into your skin. Releasing these muscles can be enough to bring instant radiance, and there are also effective off-the-shelf beauty balms.

520
Check your expression
Whenever you remember (and especially during periods of intense concentration), check whether you have slipped into bad facial habits. Are you frowning? Is your jaw clenched? Do the sides of your mouth pull downward? Don't judge, just notice, then smooth out the face to reduce tension lines.

521
Relax your face
Relaxing the face can be enough to soften frown and tension lines. Sit or lie comfortably and close your eyes. Take your thoughts away from outside matters – focus on your breathing or count to four as you breathe in and out. Consciously relax common areas of tension: drop your shoulders away from your ears, loosen your jaw, iron out your brow, feel your eyes heavy in their sockets, let your lips loosen, unclench your teeth and let your tongue lie quietly on your palate. Let your nostrils and ears become quiet. Imagine the hair follicles on the back of your head relaxing. Remain expressionless, breathing quietly through your nose, for 3–5 minutes.

522
Anti-frown tips
To prevent scowl lines and crow's feet, keep eyes relaxed at all times, even when smiling. If you have dry eyes caused by computer work, central heating and contact lenses, top up your intake of antioxidant vitamins with supplements.

523
Quick forehead release
To reduce the sight of a creased forehead make your index and middle fingers into a V-shape. Place them at the centre of your forehead and gradually stretch the fingers apart to smooth away lines. Move outwards and repeat.

524
Wear your shades
Whenever you step out into bright daylight slip on your shades (see No. 546) to prevent squinting.

525
Off-the-shelf treatments
Jurlique's best-selling anti-ageing Herbal Recovery Gel, or face-lift in a bottle, magically tightens and lifts sagging skin, brightening and restoring radiance instantly – it contains a protective screen of OPCs and other plant-derived antioxidants. The Organic Pharmacy's Expression Treatment is an all-natural organic "filler" and skin plumper.

526
Use blusher
When you look pallid, judicious application of blusher helps. To find a natural-looking colour, pinch your cheek – try to match the tone that appears. Smile to pinpoint the plump apple of the cheek, then apply blusher here and work outwards.

527
Make-up rescues
Don't be tempted to apply a thick layer of foundation on bad days. This creates a mask-like effect, and allows pigment to crease in

wrinkles and laughter lines. For a more flattering look, use light-reflecting concealer, under-eye reflectors and sheer foundation or tinted moisturizer, blending where most help is needed – beneath the eyes, around the lips, on blemishes and around age spots. Leave parts of the face bare.

528
Colour therapy

For instant radiance, rethink the colours you wear on eyes, lips, cheeks and face with each changing season. Summer, winter, and even autumn and spring call for different tones, and colouring changes after the menopause make reviews of foundation especially important. A good rule of thumb for constant renewal is never to buy the same tone of lipstick twice.

529
Give in to gravity

Lie on your front, legs wider than hip-width apart with toes pointing outwards, head resting on your hands or turned to one side. Close your eyes and relax completely towards the ground. Let your pelvis, shoulders and heels sink and your breastbone slump. Feel the skin on your face loosen, giving in to gravity. After three minutes or so, roll onto your back. Again feel the heaviness of your pelvis and shoulders. Let the weight of your head sink towards the floor. Let your skin be expressionless and heavy, moulding to the relaxed skeleton beneath it. Feel as if your pores are open, your skin receptive and clear. When you get up, try to retain this sense of clarity and freedom from set expressions.

530
Yoga inversions for instant glow

Poses that boost circulation impart an instant youthful bloom. There's no better way to do this than by inverting yourself to bring a flow of freshly oxygenated blood to the upper body.

1 Downward dog: start on your hands and knees, with feet hip-width apart. Spread your hands and press the palms and fingers into the floor. Inhaling, tuck your toes under and stretch your bottom towards the ceiling.

2 Try to straighten your legs. Keep your arms straight and imagine stretching your armpits towards your knees. Exhale to come out of the pose. Repeat three times. (Avoid this pose if you have high blood pressure.)

Scalpel-free face-lifts

Cosmetic surgery and treatments may appear to be booming but lots of women prefer a non-invasive, natural approach. Holistic facials combining massage and acupressure techniques with antioxidant oils and botanical extracts ease tension, encourage circulation and lymph drainage, and restore a youthful bloom. These treatments are quick, leave no scars and, unlike botox, make sure your face stays lively and full of expression.

531

Fingertip face-lift

The massage treatment known as Rejuvanessence®, created by holistic massage therapist and former nurse Margareta Loughran, aims to bring about a more "alive" or expressive appearance, in contrast to the "surprised" expression and fixed look of some surgical lifts. Using a press, hold and release technique, therapists work to free tension in connective tissue and facial muscle to restore flexibility and soften stress lines. Although results are discernible after one treatment, a course of six one-hour sessions is recommended.

532

Try acupuncture

Plenty of celebrities advocate cosmetic acupuncture, in which hair-fine needles are inserted as an alternative to botox. Effects include a reduction in fine wrinkles and folds on the face, lifting of sagging eyelids, and improved muscle tone and collagen production. This technique works on individual imbalances and weaknesses to regulate flow of qi energy and stimulate the body's innate healing processes. A block of 12–24 weekly treatments is advised for best results, with monthly top-up sessions to maintain the look for years.

533

Reiki for face and hands

This 15-minute non-invasive self-treatment system is taught at one-day workshops and summer schools and is said not only to refresh skin on the face and soften signs of ageing, but to alleviate signs of ageing on the hands. It teaches how to focus reiki energy to restore natural energy flow and also demonstrates facial exercises and self-massage.

534

Ko bi do rebalance

Not concerned merely with the skin, Japanese facial massage, or Ko bi do, aims to rejuvenate by working on the lifeforce known as ki. As well as offering the usual cleansing and moisturizing, this type of facial applies finger pressure to tsubos, acupoints, on the face to stimulate energy pathways, known as meridians, and to rebalance internal organs and body systems, including the nervous system.

535

Enjoy a grape break

French beauty pioneer of *vinothérapie*, Caudalie offers grape cures at the chateau on its wine estate in Bordeaux, in California and in Italy, Paris, Spain and Taiwan. Reap the anti-ageing

Grapes are used in *Vinothérapie*, a French anti-ageing beauty treatment.

benefits of the concentrated antioxidant properties of the grape vine by booking a Red Vine or Barrel Bath, Honey and Wine or Merlot Wrap, Crushed Cabernet Scrub or Sauvignon Massage.

536
Ayurveda treatments

Ayurvedic beauty treatments for vata-type skin (thinning and dry) use warming and moisturizing oils and herbal compresses. Treatments work on marma points – energy-junctions sited around the body. Pressure stimulation clears energy blockages and helps prana, lifeforce, circulate freely. This brings fresher skin and is thought to develop spiritual insight.

537
Mirror finish

Elemis' anti-ageing Visible Brilliance facial has been shown in clinical trials to increase skin elasticity by up to 28 per cent and improve moisture levels by up to 38 per cent – in just 75 minutes. Massage with moringa oil – 1700 per cent more antioxidant than other oils used cosmetically – includes Thai techniques and Tui Na movements to encourage lymphatic drainage and define the jaw line. It also includes a mask rich in cell-regenerating minerals, vitamins and plant nutrients said to make skin look visibly plumper.

Emergency eye action

From our 30s onwards, the fragile skin around the eyes starts to take on a darker hue, to droop under gravity, and to crinkle more easily. Frowning, squinting and rubbing all take their toll, and the morning after a big night out can leave the face looking noticeably older. Since the eyes are the part of the body with which we interact most with others, attention paid here can be transforming agewise.

538
Organic eye creams

Jurlique's Eye Gel is impressively firming, cooling and visibly lifts dark circles within hours. It contains antioxidant extracts of green tea, turmeric and grape seed; arnica to kickstart a sluggish circulation; and eyebright to soothe inflammation. Weleda's Intensive Eye Cream is based on oils rich in vitamins and moisture-preserving essential fatty acids, plus botanical extracts to counter puffiness. The Organic Pharmacy Lifting Eye Gel with rose hip and bilberry is recommended to deal with dark circles resulting from late nights and long-haul flights.

539
Quick pick-me-up

Apply a firming natural eye gel for a quick pick-me-up at any time of day when you feel old or when sleep beckons.

540
Clever concealers

Choose light-reflective under-eye concealers to veil dark rings. Place a dot where the inner eye meets the nose, and use a subtle brush of light-reflecting highlighter to bounce light off the brow bone at the outer edge of the eye and high on the cheekbones. But before going down the make-up route, check out what a good eye cream can do.

541
Eye oils

Since it contains few oil glands, the sensitive skin around the eyes becomes much drier with age and demands cosmetic oils that are mild, easily absorbed and free from potentially irritating fragrance. Try using a tiny amount of jojoba or sweet almond oil – these are light, yet especially nourishing for dry skin.

Apply eye oils with the soft pad of your ring finger to help combat under-eye circles.

542
Apply sparingly

When using eye oils and serums, apply a small amount using light strokes with the soft pad of your ring finger – the index finger is too strong and may drag delicate skin.

543
Rethink eye colours

If brows and lashes start to fade in colour as you get older, rethink your make-up. Mascara may need to come down a shade, to stone or grey perhaps, or have lashes dyed professionally. Shaping with eyelash curlers gives a wide-eyed look. Avoid circling the eyes with liner and eye pencils, which can drag on mature skin.

544
Reduce creasing

To prevent creased eye make-up, use eye serum on the lids. Allow to dry for 4–5 minutes before applying a very thin layer of foundation followed by a dusting of face powder. Only then add a thin layer of eyeshadow.

545
Sleep upright

To ensure rested eyes the night before a big event, sleep upright on pillows and apply cold compresses to the eye area.

546
Protect against UV

UV radiation can contribute to degenerative eye diseases and cataracts. Choose sunglasses that guarantee full UV protection and wear them everywhere. Polarized lenses are best for reducing glare. For greater levels of protection choose snug-fitting, large-framed glasses or opt for space-age wraparounds.

547
Naturopathic cure

Naturopaths might suggest puffiness beneath the eyes is the result of fluid retention, indicating that the liver and kidneys aren't working as efficiently as they could. To make a difference, cut out alcohol and processed foods for a couple of weeks, eat more vegetables, drink water, and take exercise to kickstart circulation. Also set aside time for destressing.

548
Cooling compresses

Tighten under-eye skin and reduce inflammation by placing chilled camomile, green or black teabags or slices of cucumber beneath the eyes. Relax for 10–15 minutes.

549
Eating for eye health

Introduce lots of vitamin C and colourful carotenoids into your diet. Find vitamin C in strawberries, oranges and mangoes, carotenoids in orange and dark green coloured fruit and vegetables. In studies at a Boston university, such a diet was associated with greatly reduced risk of cataracts in over 50s. Don't forget sources of vitamin E, calcium and zinc, too, associated in other studies with a significant reduction in risk of age-related macular degeneration, the main cause of blindness post 55.

550
Weight-train your eyes

Keeping your eyes closed and relaxed, lashes resting on cheeks, raise your eyebrows. If you find this difficult, rest your index finger lightly over the lashes. Hold for five, then lower the eyebrows slowly. Repeat 3 times. Lightly rest your index fingers horizontally across the under-eye area, above the cheeks.

Cucumber refreshes skin around the eyes.

Try to lift the weight of the fingers by lifting the under-eye muscles without engaging other parts of the eye. Repeat three sets of five lifts.

551
Banish crow's feet

Place the tips of your ring fingers between your eyebrows. Circle down the nose and out over the cheekbones. Sweep up to the temples and to the centre of the forehead. Repeat, circling for 30 seconds. **Take the eyebrows** between thumbs and index fingers, starting in the centre. Pinch and roll, moving towards the outer eye. Circle the temples with your ring fingers. Exerting a little pressure, open and close the eyes rapidly.

552
Brow-shaping

An expert brow beautician can take years off your look, adding lift and lightness to the eye area by judicious plucking and shaping. Book a six-monthly appointment and ask for advice on keeping brows in check between times.

Brow shaping by an expert beautician can add lift and lightness to your eyes.

Lip treatments

One of the most obvious tell-tale signs of ageing is a "bleeding" of lip colour into fine wrinkles around the mouth. Exercises and make-up know-how can help prevent or minimize this age-old giveaway.

553
Off-the-shelf lip balms

Look for edible salves made from honey and nourishing food-quality organic oils and waxes and lipsticks coloured with pigment from earth minerals rather than coal tar dyes. Try Dr Hauschka, Aveda and Lavera, Jurlique or Living Nature. Green People have created the first certified organic lipstick.

554
Avoid the filler look

To prevent make-up collecting in fine lines around the mouth, open your mouth and pull your lips over your teeth. Drop the bottom jaw, then lift several times. Release the lips, then puff out the skin around the cheeks and mouth before applying foundation or face powder.

555
Define lips

Before applying lipstick apply foundation and a light dusting of face powder. Outline lips on your natural lip line (never outside) with a lip pencil that matches your lip colour. Fill in with lipstick or gloss, blotting to remove excess colour that might be prone to bleeding.

556
Plumping exercise

With lips and mouth closed, smile widely, hold, then pucker the lips. Holding the kiss shape, raise the top lip towards your nose. Hold. Keeping the same mouth shape, draw your lips in tightly around your teeth and hold. Repeat five times.

557
Glossy trick

Dot a little lip gloss or a slightly darker shade of lip colour in the centre of your lower lip and blend outward for plumper-looking lips.

558
Eating for soft lips

When skin on the lips becomes cracked, build more B vitamins into your diet in the form of green leafy vegetables, pulses, whole grains and yeast extract.

Outline your lips with a lip pencil to give clear definition before applying lipstick.

Essential toothcare

Research is showing that people with gum disease have a raised risk of heart attack later in life. Built-up plaque is the most common cause of gum disease and tooth decay, so for maximum anti-ageing benefits, revisit your daily brushing and flossing regime. The cosmetic effect is important, too: yellowing teeth are a give-away of age.

559
Holistic dentistry

If you can find a holistic dentist, he or she will examine your head and neck as well as your teeth, and look at the impact your diet and lifestyle have on your dental health, working with you to eliminate potential problems. Holistic and homeopathic dentists may use homeopathic remedies and essential oils to relax and ease pain and prescribe herbs to support immunity or offer acupuncture or hypnosis for pain reduction.

560
Go electric

Research suggests electric toothbrushes with oscillating brushes that rotate in two directions are more effective at removing plaque and reducing gum inflammation than regular toothbrushes. Change the head regularly, according to the manufacturer's instructions. Brush at least twice a day for a minimum of two minutes. Pay attention to the area where gums and teeth meet, circling gently at front and back.

561
Don't forget to floss

Without flossing you miss out on cleaning 40 per cent of the surface area of your teeth. Daily flossing helps you clean the parts of the teeth where disease often starts: the gumline. If your gums are prone to bleeding, you need to floss more. Use light pressure, adopting a zig-zag technique and easing under the gumline.

562
Destress daily

Studies show that stress can aggravate gum disease, making the mouth more acidic – another factor in tooth decay. Aim to build relaxation stops into your day: a yoga class, 5 minutes for meditation, a brisk lunchtime walk.

563
All-round nutrient

Take a combination of the tissue salts Silica, Nat.Mur and Calc Phos, a good all-round micro-nutrient for keeping teeth and gums healthy. This is particularly good if you have sensitive teeth or sore gums.

564
Prevent yellowing

Smoking is a prime cause of yellowing, but some people also like to avoid rich-coloured food and drink, such as black coffee and red wine. However, antioxidants in red wine may help prevent gum disease according to one study. To prevent yellowing worsening, have your teeth cleaned by a professional every six months. Don't use commercial whiteners – bleaching agents can irritate inflamed gums.

565
Gum-care tips

The expression "long in the tooth" alludes to the fact that gums tend to recede with age, making the front teeth appear longer. Luckily this is optional if you care for gums well. Bleeding gums might indicate gum disease or tooth decay, so have them checked out by a dentist. You might like to take a supplement of Co-enzyme Q_{10} (see No. 173), which is thought to promote periodontal healing. Make sure you are getting enough anti-inflammatory vitamin D from exposure to sunshine and from eating salmon and mackerel. In one study people with highest levels of vitamin D were 20 per cent less likely to suffer from bleeding gums.

566
Massage the gums

Morning and night after brushing, massage the gums with fingertips, making small circular rotations over the front and back.

567
Treating mouth ulcers

Gargle with salt water, add 1–2ml myrrh tincture to a glass of water and rinse. Eat bio-yogurt daily. If a

Cranberry juice is cavity preventing.

mouth ulcer does not clear up within two weeks, have it checked by your doctor.

568
Soothe sore gums

If you have receding or sore gums that bleed easily, the homeopathic remedy Carbo.Veg 6c could help. Take daily for a few weeks and visit a homeopathic dentist.

569
Drink cranberry juice

This juice contains a chemical that prevents cavity-causing bacteria from sticking to teeth, suggests a recent study. Look for brands low in sugar and artificial sweeteners.

570
Shut your mouth

Always breathe through the nose rather than the mouth: the nose acts as a filter to potentially harmful airborne particles and bacteria. Mouth breathing dries the gums and leads to bad breath. Remind yourself to shut your mouth every time you look at your watch or save at the computer. Exercises can help. Pay attention to where your tongue lies naturally: it should sit against the roof of the mouth at rest and when swallowing. See also that your upper lip drops heavily onto your upper gums, weighting down the

teeth. If you suspect age-related drooping of cartilage in your nose is affecting your breathing, visit your doctor.

571
Breath-freshening rinse

Gargle once daily with this rinse to keep your breath fresh.

1 tsp salt
500mg vitamin C capsule

Dissolve the salt in warm water. Stir in the contents of the capsule.

572
Antiseptic mouthwash

Stir 2 drops essential oil of tea tree and 1 drop essential oil of grapefruit into ½ tsp sweet almond oil. Whisk into a pint of water. Rinse and spit out (do not swallow).

Homemade antiseptic mouthwash keeps breath fresh.

573
White tea for cavity prevention

Drinking white tea is particularly good for preventing tooth cavities and destroying the bacteria that can cause pneumonia, studies suggest.

574
Getting rid of amalgam

Mercury, a component of amalgam fillings, has been linked to health issues from headaches, mouth ulcers and frequent sore throats to Alzheimer's. At your next check-up, ask your dentist about alternatives, such as composite fillings. When having mercury amalgam fillings removed, take the homeopathic remedy Merc.Sol 6c twice a day.

575
Confidence boosting

Porcelain veneers and crowns and realignment work can be an expensive but natural way to improve self-confidence if your smile lets you down at work and in social situations. Ask your dentist about cosmetic procedures.

576
Yummy teeth cleaners

After a meal eat a chunk of cheese to naturalize acids in the mouth that can cause tooth decay. Or eat sun-dried raisins, which contain bacteria-suppressing plant chemicals. Alternatively, finish a meal with strawberries: try to rub over teeth and gums to remove staining. Unwaxed peel of organic oranges and lemons works in a similar way.

Strawberry cleaners: rub this fruit over teeth and gums after a meal to remove stains.

577
Avoiding fluoride

Exposure to very large doses of fluoride over long periods can cause fluorosis (symptoms include brittle bones and hypothyroidism). Some nutritionists worry that fluoride interferes with up-take of calcium, magnesium, iron and zinc. If your water supply is fluoridated, you might prefer to use a toothpaste without fluoride.

578
Off-the-shelf natural toothpastes

Conventional toothpastes may contain chemicals you prefer to avoid. Try Weleda's Plant Gel Toothpaste, formulated to be gentle on delicate gums or Green People's Citrus Toothpaste with antioxidant vitamin C and aloe vera to tackle swelling. Weleda's Salt Toothpaste is an intense cleaning experience no other preparation can compete with.

Natural bathing

Nothing is quite as stress-beating as a soak in a warm bath with uplifting or relaxing scents and a skin-softening blend of oils. When skin is very dry, an oil bath is helpful because skin softened by water and warmth absorbs nutritious oils more effectively. Mineral salts help relieve aching muscles and joints and revive tired skin. (See page 2 for cautions.)

579
Get the temperature right

Heat and cold can have as much effect on body and mind as the botanicals and oils you choose to throw into a bath. Take a warm bath to soothe, relax and relieve aching muscles. Cool water baths are more invigorating, refreshing and revitalizing, while cold water jets tone the skin. Avoid very hot baths: they can be exhausting, dehydrate the body and dry out skin.

580
Mineral detox

Mineral salts have a detoxifying action, encouraging perspiration to carry away waste products.

9 tbsp Epsom salts
4 tbsp sea salt
3 drops each essential oils
  of cypress and juniper
1 tsp olive oil

Blend the salts in a bowl, then stir into a very warm bath. Just before stepping in, mix the essential oils into the olive oil and swish in. Bathe for 12 minutes for best effects. Sip a glass of water. Shower off salt residue before retiring to bed. (Avoid if you are pregnant, have heart or kidney disease or high blood pressure.)

581
Flower bath

Combine jasmine and rose oils to create a soothing, yet uplifting bathing experience.

6 drops essential oil of jasmine
2 drops essential oil of rose
1 tsp sweet almond oil
2 tbsp rosewater
rose petals or jasmine flowers

Drop the essential oils into the almond oil. Swish the rosewater and oil mixture into the bath and throw in the petals just before stepping in. Place a strainer over the drain when emptying the bathwater.

582
Vanilla milk revitalizer

For smooth, revitalized skin, cast two vanilla pods into the water as the bath fills. Place 12 tbsp milk

A mineral salt bath before bed detoxifies the body.

powder in a bowl and dilute with double the amount of cool water, adding the liquid gradually until no lumps remain, then pour into the bath. After bathing, rinse the vanilla pods and reserve for another bath.

583
Coconut milk bath
This nourishing creamy mix rehydrates the skin and incorporates the benefits of antioxidant honey.

small can coconut milk
1 tbsp buckwheat honey
2 drops each essential oils of vetivert and geranium

Blend the coconut milk, honey and essential oils together. Stir into a running bath just before stepping in.

584
Summer herb soak
Gather two handfuls each of fresh lavender stalks and fresh leafy mint stems. Tie in a posy and throw into a hot bath as it fills. Scatter the leaves of 4-6 scented roses into the water before stepping in.

585
White tea bath
Make the most of the antioxidant properties of white tea.

4 white tea bags
2 tsp sweet almond oil

Soothing and uplifting: enjoy a flower bath when you are in need of a boost.

Boil a kettle of water, and leave to cool slightly. Place the tea bags in a teapot and pour over the hot water. Leave to steep as you run a bath, pouring in the oil. Before stepping in, pour in the tea infusion and swish to disperse. Close your eyes, placing the cooled, squeezed tea bags over them.

586
Seaweed boost
Restore vibrancy to the skin while detoxifying and boosting circulation.

2 large strips dried kelp or other seaweed
6 tbsp dried mint
12 tbsp seaweed-flecked sea salt

Crumble the seaweed into a large pan of water and add the mint. Bring to a boil, cover and simmer for 30 minutes. Add the salt to a body-temperature bath, then pour in the seaweed mixture. After bathing,

place a strainer over the drain and shower off remaining salt. Drink a glass of water. (Avoid if you have heart or blood pressure problems or are pregnant.)

587
Sandalwood meditation
Combine these oils to produce a bath made for meditation.

5 drops essential oil of sandalwood
2 drops essential oil of patchouli
2 tsp sweet almond oil
sandalwood incense and soap
tealight

Run a warm bath. Just before stepping in, mix the essential oils into the almond oil and pour into the bath, swishing to disperse. Light the incense and a tealight placed at the end of the bath. Wash with the sandalwood soap. Without blinking, focus on the tip of the tealight's flame, trying to find the point where it disappears. When you can look no longer, close your eyes and see the image in your mind's eye.

588
Soothing bath bag
Spoon 12 tbsp milk powder and 12 tbsp oatmeal into the centre of a large square of muslin, then tie the corners in the centre to secure. Place in a bath as you run the water, then use as a soap substitute to cleanse and relieve irritated skin.

589

Relaxing bath oil

Combine these essential oils for soothing effects on body and mind.

1 tsp sweet almond oil
4 drops essential oil of lavender
3 drops essential oil of camomile
2 drops essential oil of geranium

Mix the oils and swish into bathwater just before stepping in.

590

Detoxifying bath oil

When you need some "get up and go" try this zesty, woody aroma.

1 tsp grapeseed oil
4 drops essential oil of cypress
2 drops each essential oils of juniper and rosemary

Mix the oils and swish into bathwater just before stepping in. (Omit rosemary oil if you have epilepsy; juniper if you have kidney disease.)

591

Reviving bath oil

These essential oils are renowned for their purifying properties.

1 tsp sunflower oil
4 drops essential oil of rose

2 drops essential oil of orange
2 drops essential oil of rosemary

Mix the oils and swish into bathwater just before stepping in. (Omit rosemary oil if you have epilepsy.)

592

Hand bathing

Take half a bottle of red wine and bring to the boil with a handful each of nettles, rosemary, thyme and mint. Allow to simmer for 20 minutes, covered. When cool, strain and use to bathe the hands to boost circulation and prevent swelling.

593

Spiced bath bag

Stimulating and invigorating, yet sensual, this wonderful mix of spices is great for enhancing a long soak in a wintertime bath.

- 2 sticks cinnamon, broken
- 3 bay leaves
- 2 tsp cloves, crushed
- 1 tsp grated nutmeg
- 1 tsp black peppercorns, crushed

1 Pile all the ingredients in the centre of a piece of muslin and tie the corners to secure.

2 Suspend beneath the hot tap while you fill the bath or float the bag in the water. (Avoid during pregnancy.)

594
Add moisture

Customize any dry skin bath oil mix by adding a teaspoon of avocado or wheatgerm oil or one vitamin E capsule (prick and squeeze in).

595
Natural soap

Search out best-quality sandalwood soap, which always comes from Mysore in India. Relish the texture and intense scent, thought to promote meditation and valued in India for its cooling effect.

596
Take a sauna

Japanese research suggests a 15-minute daily sauna can help prevent heart disease. As searing heat causes blood vessels to dilate, blood flow increases to the skin's surface; and blood pressure drops. (Avoid if you have high blood pressure, heart or vascular disease, varicose veins, or if you are pregnant.)

597
Sea bathing

Whenever the opportunity arises bathe outdoors – in the ocean, in mountain springs, in naturally heated spring water, in mud baths, beneath waterfalls – to benefit the mind and increase wellbeing.

Revitalizing body buffs

Exfoliation loosens the top layer of dead skin cells, speeding the skin's natural process of regeneration to bring about a youthful glow. It also allows for better penetration of oils and herbs, which impart nourishment as well as a lustre to the skin. Body clays are super-effective on ageing skin, replenishing by imparting minerals and trace elements as they dry. (Avoid full-body masks during pregnancy.)

598
Use natural ingredients

There's evidence that the environment and marine life suffer when non-biodegradable granules from commercially available exfoliators head down the drain. Use only natural, degradable (and edible) products to exfoliate, such as salt, sugar and pepper, rice, oatmeal and sesame seeds.

599
Upward strokes

When massaging in body scrubs make long strokes always in the direction of the heart. Improving circulation maximizes the availability of oxygen and nutrients and primes the organs of elimination to carry away waste products. Use a circular scrubbing action over areas that need more attention, such as the heels, knees, elbows and areas of cellulite.

Hemp oil nourishes the skin.

600
Sweet and salt buff

Oils give the skin a lustre that remains after showering.

1 tbsp sea salt
1 tbsp brown sugar
1 tbsp hemp oil
1 tbsp avocado oil
4 drops essential oil of peppermint

Combine the salt and sugar in a bowl. Stir in enough of the oils to make a thick paste. Drop in the essential oil. Rub handfuls into the skin. Shower off. (If you have sensitive skin or are breastfeeding omit the essential oil.)

601
Mud and banana body mask

This full body treat feels really indulgent – enjoy!

1 ripe banana
1 tbsp fine oatmeal
4 tbsp kaolin clay
2 tbsp rosewater
4 drops essential oil of rose

Mash the banana and mix into the oatmeal in a large bowl. Stir in the dry clay, then little by little mix in the rosewater and enough warm water to make a smooth paste. Finally, mix in the essential oil. Coat the body. Relax in a warm room for 15 minutes, until dry, then wipe away with warm wet face cloths. Take a cool shower and drink a glass of water.

602
Aftersun mask

Help your skin recover from sun exposure with this soothing mask.

4 organic carrots, grated
2 tbsp runny honey
1 tbsp wheatgerm oil
4 drops essential oil of lavender
2 drops essential oil of carrot seed

Mix together the grated carrot with the honey and wheatgerm oil. Stir in the essential oils. Rub handfuls over the skin to cool and impart moisture. Work gently into areas of soreness. Wipe away with warm face cloths and then take a cool shower.

Natural cellulite busters

Unsightly dimpling of the skin around the buttocks, hips and thighs is increasingly common after the age of 30. Loss of skin elasticity and resilience contributes, as does thinning of the top layer of skin and reduced firmness in the fibres that connect skin to muscle.

603
Firm loose skin

Homeopaths often recommend the tissue salt Calc Fluor to pregnant women as it enhances tissue elasticity, particularly the skin, but if you had your children some time ago, it's not too late. Try taking Calc Fluor three times daily alongside your exercise regime to firm up loose skin and reduce stretch marks.

604
Softening lumpiness

Silica tissue salts can help to soften lumpy or hardened tissue if taken over a long period of time. This is especially helpful for any lumpiness of tissue remaining after an injury or surgery. Take two tablets up to four times daily over several months.

605
Flower remedies

Try the Australian Bush Flower Essence combination recommended for cellulite – Bottlebrush, Dagger Hakea and Billy Goat Plum, taken together. Take 6 drops morning and evening for two weeks.

606
Anti-cellulite massage oil

This works better if you also take up exercise and give up smoking.

2 tbsp (colourless) sesame oil
3 drops each essential oils of
  rosemary and lavender
2 drops essential oil of juniper

Blend the oils, then massage into hips, abdomen, buttocks and thighs, using firm kneading movements to lift and squeeze the flesh. Rotate your knuckles all over the area, then finish with flowing upward strokes. Repeat morning and night. (Omit rosemary oil if you have epilepsy; juniper if you have kidney disease.)

607
Hot and cold shower

At the end of a shower, turn the water as cold as you dare and shoot it in the direction of your cellulite.

Make large then small circles with the shower head. Increase the temperature to very warm and repeat. End with a blast of cold.

608

Circulation boosting exercise

For firmness in the legs and butt, focus on exercises that spot-train the muscles of the thighs and buttocks: squats, lunges, stepping, squat thrusts. Follow with yoga poses to stretch and lengthen these muscles.

609

Birch swatches

In Russia, the traditional tonic for the skin and circulation is a "'whisking" with a leafy swatch of birch in the steamy banya, or bathhouse, promoting circulation and elimination in specific areas of the body. Birch extract has a purifying action and it is often used in anti-cellulite oil blends. It is also thought to be effective for arthritis, rheumatism and very dry skin conditions. Try to replicate the Russian effect in a steamy bathroom with a bunch of leafy birch twigs.

610

Off-the-shelf products

Try Weleda's Birch Cellulite Oil: extracts from the leaves of organically grown silver birch trees

contain flavonoids that encourage the body to give up and flush away toxins. Massage twice a day into slightly damp skin.

611

Skin brushing

Before a morning shower or before applying anti-cellulite oils, dry brush your skin for five minutes. Start by making long strokes with a loofah or body brush up the legs, arms and torso, always working towards the heart. Then brush briskly up the front and back of the thighs, buttocks, upper arms (move gently over the breasts and underarm area) and back. Make clockwise circles over the abdomen to stimulate digestion.

Oiling the body

Massaging oils into damp skin after a bath or shower gives the body extra opportunities to absorb vitamin- and mineral-rich antioxidant fruit and vegetable oils. In Ayurveda it is believed to draw toxins to the surface of the skin and to amplify peace of mind, contributing to longevity. See guidelines for using oils on page 2.

Extra-virgin olive oil makes a good carrier massage oil.

- irritated skin: jojoba, hemp and extra-virgin olive oils
- inflamed skin: jojoba and extra-virgin olive oils
- sun-damaged skin: grapeseed, olive, wheatgerm and rosehip oils

Use only the oils specified, being careful to heed the cautions that apply to individual recipes.

614

Go organic

Look for organic cold-pressed oils (nutrients can be lost in heat treatment) sold in dark glass bottles. Ethically sourced oils from small projects that protect environment and workers are best. Supermarkets and whole food stores are as good a source as beauty emporia.

615

Calming body oil

Blend 3 drops each essential oils of lavender, geranium and camomile into 4 tbsp sweet almond oil to create this soothing body oil.

616

Invigorating body oil

Blend 4 drops essential oil of grapefruit, 3 drops essential oil of geranium and 2 drops essential oil of juniper into 4 tbsp sweet almond oil. (Omit juniper oil if you have kidney problems; grapefruit oil if exposing skin to sun.)

612

Aromatherapy oils

Essential oils have the ability to act on specific body systems as well as on the emotions and mind. But they are too concentrated to be used directly on the skin. Dilute a few drops in a larger amount of a carrier oil:

613

Blending rules

Choose a carrier oil according to your skin type:
- dry skin: sesame seed, avocado, sweet almond oil
- delicate skin: apricot kernel, sunflower seed oil

617

Moroccan secrets

Look out for argan oil extracted from the seeds of a Moroccan tree. Highly prized for its anti-wrinkle and skin-softening benefits, it helps counter the ravages of sun and wind. This oil is rich in antioxidants – it contains double the amount of tocophenols and almost twice as much sun-saving vitamin E as olive oil. Massage into dry and scarred skin or dab onto pimples and acne.

618

Elasticity balm

To soften scars and promote elasticity, mix 4 drops each essential oils of jasmine and lavender plus 2 drops essential oil of mandarin into 4 tbsp extra-virgin olive or argan oil. (Omit mandarin oil if exposing skin to the sun.)

Lavender oil has a relaxing, calming effect.

Natural pedicure

Feet frequently bear the brunt of everyday stressors, as we rely on them to carry us through the day, and often expect them to look good in heels as they do so. The tension this creates can show on our faces, in frown lines and stress headaches. So, reviving the feet can act like a mini face-lift, bringing about an impression of rest and softer features.

619

Dry skin serum

Massage this serum into flaking or hard skin or nails.

2 tbsp sesame seed oil
1 tsp wheatgerm oil
2 drops each essential oils of
   sandalwood and myrrh

Pour the oils into a clean, dark glass bottle. Drop in the essential oils. Lid and store in a dark, cool place. Shake before use. To apply, massage into especially dry areas on the feet.

620

Fruity treat

What could be more luxurious than enveloping tired feet in fruit?

½ pineapple, peeled
½ papaya, peeled
juice of 1 lime

Blitz the fruit in a blender, then mix in the lime juice. Spread the paste over both feet. Place each foot in a plastic bag and envelope in warm towels for 10 minutes. Step into a warm foot bath to wash off.

621

Aching foot bath

Use this to revive the feet and soften hardened skin.

4 drops essential oil of tea tree
3 drops essential oil of cypress
2 tsp jojoba oil

Mix the essential oils into the jojoba. Stir into a bucket of warm water. Plunge in the feet and legs and relax for 5–10 minutes. To finish, step into a bucket of cold water containing a cup of green tea.

622

Salt and pepper polish

Combat cracking dry skin with a peppy polish.

1 tbsp sea salt
1 tsp finely ground black pepper
2.5 cm (1 in) fresh ginger root, grated
1 tbsp runny honey
1 tsp extra-virgin olive oil

Mix together the salt and pepper in a bowl. Add the grated ginger and mix to a paste with the honey. Stir in the olive oil. Massage into hard skin on the heels and balls of the foot. Plunge feet into a warm foot bath to wash off.

623

Peppermint leg reviver

The essential oils in this blend are cooling and pain relieving.

2 tbsp jojoba oil
1 tsp wheatgerm oil
4 drops essential oil of peppermint
2 drops essential oil of cypress

Stir together the jojoba and wheatgerm oil. Drop in the essential oils of peppermint and cypress. Massage into feet and legs using long, smooth upward strokes.

624

Off-the-shelf intensive care

Burt's Bees peppermint-scented Coconut Foot Crème is an extremely effective night treatment for very dry cracked feet – it also smells delicious. Spiezia Organics' Organic Foot Balm has a unique consistency and brings lasting softness to the feet.

Give yourself a bedtime foot massage to encourage deep sleep.

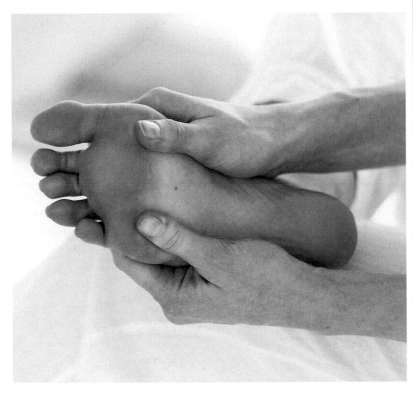

625

Home pedicure

Remove nail polish from your toetails by sweeping acetone-free remover, working from cuticle to tip, then place your feet in a foot bath for 10 minutes. Scrub gently with an exfoliator.

Dry the feet very well with a soft towel, then file your toenails with an emery board, using long strokes from the outer edges inward. Wrap a cotton ball around an orange stick and use this to ease back the cuticles.

Apply a clay or fruit mask, making sure you cover the heels and balls of the feet. Massage well into areas of dry, hard skin. Allow to dry for 10 minutes. Rinse feet and dry well. Buff with a chamois, then moisturize with oil, rubbing well into each nail.

626

Enjoy a pre-sleep foot massage

Warm some colourless sesame or olive oil. Massage into the soles of the feet and the toes, sandwiching the top and bottom of the foot between your hands. Make knuckling movements over the sole, rotate each toe, pressing at the tip, and trace the grooves on the top of the foot. Put on warmed cotton socks (zap in the microwave) and retire to bed.

Walk barefoot on pebbles to stimulate acupressure points on the soles of the feet, eliciting health benefits throughout the body.

627

Varicose vein treatment

The best topical treatment for varicose veins is witch-hazel cream or ointment. Rub on gently to soothe discomfort as well as reduce inflammation.

628

Homeopathy for varicose veins

Take the following daily for short periods of time to relieve symptoms:
• Hammamelis 30c treats inflamed, sore or itching varicose veins.
• Pulsatilla 30c helps varicose veins of legs and feet which feel cold or numb, especially after standing.
• Sepia 30c is good for women whose varicose veins arrived during pregnancy and have never got better and for tired legs and poor circulation generally.

629

Barefoot acupressure

Walking barefoot stimulates acupressure points on the soles of the feet, with health benefits throughout the body. Construct a walking path by placing in a row different sized pebbles, sticks and broom handles and balls of various dimensions. Walk along the path carefully. When you feel aches and points of tension on the sole or toes move more slowly, rolling the items around the feet and exerting pressure carefully to ease out tension and enhance mobility.

630

Cashmere cosseting

Nothing feels quite so relaxing after a hard day than slipping into a pair of cashmere socks, and this shows on the face. Carry them in your bag for instant cosseting in any situation, at work, after wearing heels, while camping. If you can afford it, invest in mood-enhancing colours: red and orange promote creativity and zest for life while tones of green and blue have a relaxing effect.

631

Try the yoga "legs up the wall" pose

Try this rejuvenating posture before a pedicure or foot massage, whenever your feet ache or to help relieve varicose veins. Find a good clear wall space. Curl up on your side with your bottom close to the wall, then swing your legs so that they end up vertical, heels resting on the wall. If your legs cannot straighten, wriggle your bottom away from the wall until they are comfortable. Close your eyes and relax for up to 10 minutes.

Non-toxic manicure

No matter how well we look after the skin on our faces, our hands betray our age. Wrinkles and protruding veins result from decades of exposure to extremes of temperature, hot and cold water, and pursuits such as gardening, cleaning and DIY. After the menopause, skin on the palms may thicken and be prone to cracking. Nails suffer, too, becoming more brittle, ridged, opaque or dull. And post 55, age spots become more common.

632

Nasty nail polish

Three ingredients found in many nail polishes are suspected to be harmful to the human body. The reproductive toxin DBP (dibutyl phthalate), banned since 2004 in products sold in the European Union, still features in most US formulations. Formaldehyde is "reasonably anticipated" to be a human carcinogen states the US National Toxicology programme, and toluene adversely affects the nervous system. All three are on California's list of chemicals considered cancer-causing. Sign up to the campaign against their inclusion in nail products at www.SafeCosmetics.org.

633

Non-chip French manicure

Shape nails using an emery board, then soak fingertips in warmed full-fat milk for 10 minutes. Dry well. Rub a drop of rosehip oil into each nail. Ease back cuticles with an orange stick tipped with cotton wool to reveal the half moons. Clean beneath the nails with another cotton-wool tipped orange stick to whiten the tips. Let nails absorb any remaining oil for 10 minutes then gently buff the nail with a fine pumice stone or fine-textured buffer, working in one direction only. Finally, rub the nail with a little beeswax on a chamois until it is pink and shiny.

634

Milk and oil hand bath

Milk is a natural exfoliator; frankincense oil suits mature skin.

2 cups full-fat milk, warmed
2 drops essential oil of frankincense

Place the milk in a wide bowl, drop in the essential oil and soak hands for 5 minutes.

635

Deep-cleansing nail soak

This may help to lighten and soften yellowing nails.

juice of half a lemon
1 tsp avocado oil
1 tsp extra-virgin olive oil
2 drops essential oil of neroli

Add the lemon juice to a bowl of warm water. Stir in the oils until amalgamated well. Soak the hands for 10-15 minutes.

636

Hand scrub

Sugar dissolves in liquid, making it a gentle exfoliator.

½ cup full-fat milk, warmed
½ cup demerara sugar

Pour the milk little by little into the sugar until you have a mixture with a grainy consistency. Massage into the hands. Plunge hands into a hand bath to rinse.

637

Age-spot treatment oil

All these oils are recommended for sun-damaged skin.

1 tbsp grapeseed oil
1 tsp each rosehip and wheatgerm oils
4 drops essential oil of carrot seed
1 drop essential oil of lemon (omit for sensitive skin and before exposing skin to sun)

Combine the oils in a clean dark glass bottle. Lid and store in a cool, dark place. Shake before use, then massage into the hands.

638
Age-spot reduction mask

Use this mask once a week to soften your skin and leave it feeling more youthful.

2 tbsp kaolin
1 tbsp aloe vera gel
2 tbsp cider vinegar
2 drops essential oil of carrot seed
1 drop essential oil of neroli

Put the kaolin in a large bowl and mix in the aloe gel and enough vinegar to form a smooth paste. Drop in the essential oils. Massage over the hands, relax for 10 minutes while the mask dries, then rinse off by plunging hands into a hand bath.

639
Energizing hand massage

Warm a little oil between your palms by rubbing them together. Supporting your left palm with your right fingers, circle the middle of the palm with your thumb. Gradually widen the circle to cover the palm. **Turn the left hand over**, add more oil and slide your thumb from the base of the fingers towards the wrist, working along each channel. **Work the left thumb** and fingers from base to tip, using your right

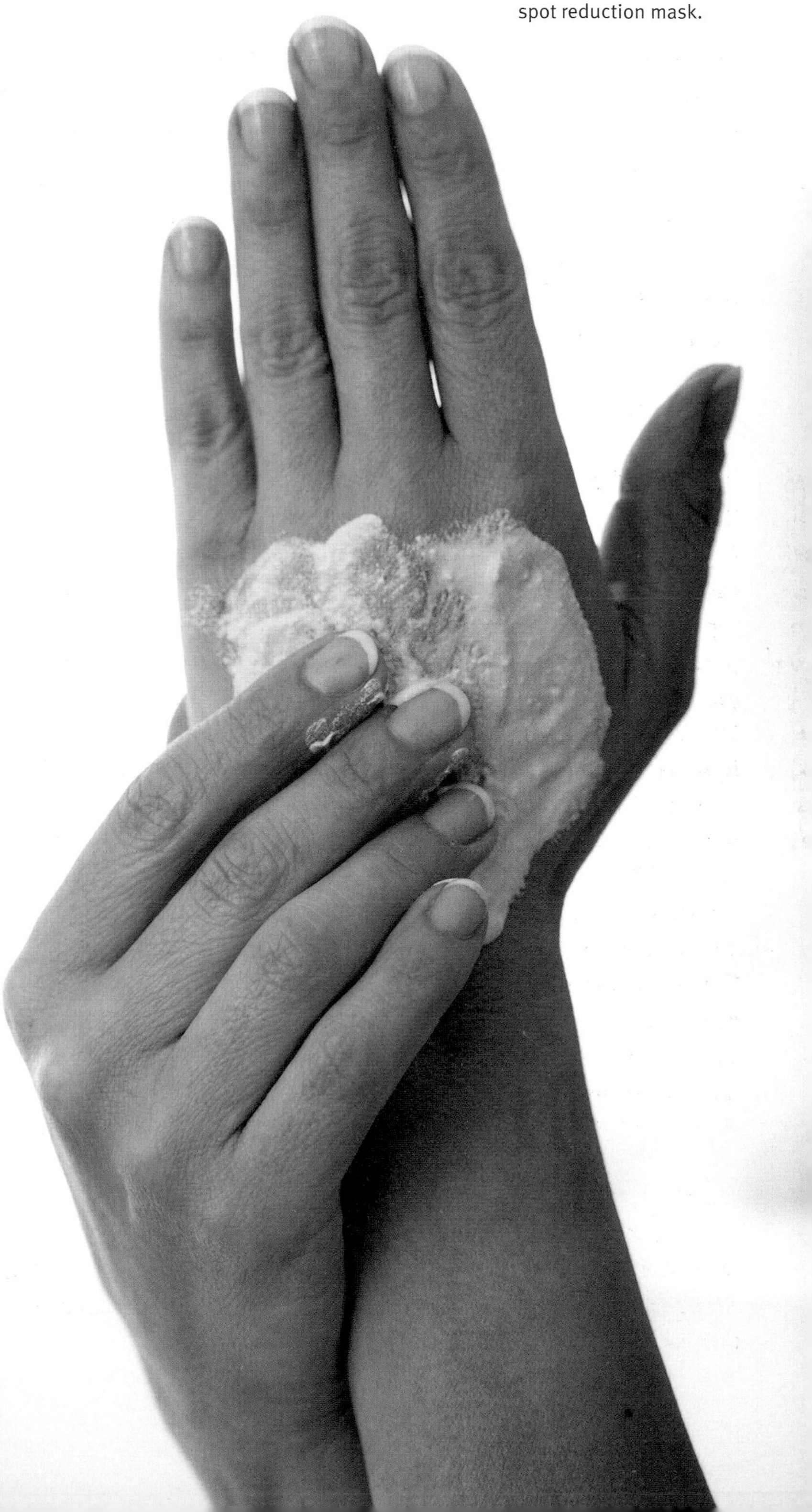

Minimize signs of ageing with an age-spot reduction mask.

thumb and index finger like a corkscrew along the length of each digit. Briefly squeeze at the tip as you pull your fingers away. Repeat the massage on the other hand.

640
Softening oil for brittle nails

This recipe is effective for toenails as well as fingernails.

1 tbsp (colourless) sesame oil
1 tsp each macadamia, avocado and
   wheatgerm oils

2 drops each essential oils of
sandalwood and frankincense

Combine the oils in a clean dark glass bottle. Lid and store in a cool, dark place. Shake before use, then massage into hands and nails.

641
Off-the-shelf care

Burt's Bees Shea Butter Hand Repair Crème protects hands prone to chapping, roughness and premature ageing with oils and botanical extracts effective at combating wrinkles and age spots.

Living Nature's Manuka Honey Hand and Body Cream doubles as a footbalm for very dry skin.

642
Night-time hand conditioning

In the build up to bedtime, rub lots of warmed (colourless) sesame oil into your hands. Place each hand in a plastic bag and cover with woollen mittens which have been warmed in the microwave. Lie down and relax for up to 10 minutes before removing the mittens and oil.

643
Step-by-step manicure

Avoid nail parlours and instead give yourself an all-natural manicure at home. In doing so you reduce your exposure to toluene, a key ingredient of nail polishes and removers, which is especially assaulting for the nervous system.

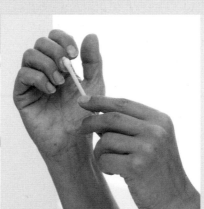

1 Remove nail polish with an acetone-free remover, sweeping from cuticle to tip. Soften hands and nails in a hand bath for 5–10 minutes. Pat dry.

2 With a cotton bud, ease out dirt from beneath each nail. Wrap a cotton ball around an orange stick and dip into rosehip oil. Ease back cuticles.

3 File nails with a soft emery board in one direction only, working from the outside inwards. Massage in a little avocado or rosehip oil.

Natural haircare basics

About one third of post-menopausal women develop hair loss or thinning. Hair grows more slowly as we age and individual strands become thinner and lost hair is less readily replaced. Longer hair may fare worse, given its extra duration of exposure to the sun, blow drying and styling products. However, establishing a good haircare routine will help keep it healthy and strong into old age.

Stimulate the scalp by brushing your hair regularly from root to tip.

644
Daily brushing

Use a clean brush to brush hair from root to tip away from the face. This stimulates the scalp, encouraging blood flow to follicles, and distributes natural oils through the length of the hair shaft.

645
Clean your brush

Once a week soak brushes and combs in shampoo and tepid water for an hour. Rinse well and allow to dry before use.

646
Get a good haircut

Stepping out from the salon with a head-turning haircut is an effortless way to take years off your look, so be sure to book appointments at least four times a year – every 6–8 weeks with a short cut. A good stylist considers your hair type and face shape, the condition your hair is in and the life you lead before cutting – and should keep doing so, suggesting changes over the years that keep you looking contemporary. If your hairdresser always gives you the same cut, try a new stylist.

647
Long or short

Many women feel short hair is the way to go as hair becomes thinner, but long hair in good condition always looks stunning. Opt for cuts with some layering to create volume and body, and with lines (a sharp bob or interesting fringe, perhaps) that draw attention away from a saggy chin or frown lines.

648
Visualization for scalp health

Sit comfortably resting palms on thighs to relax the shoulders. Close your eyes and be aware of your breath moving in and out.

Breathing in, feel the refreshing air drawn in through your nose and cool behind your eyes. Imagine it invigorating your scalp and follicles. **Exhaling,** visualize the breath moving up your spine and over the back of your head, exiting through your nose. Imagine it energizing every part of the body it touches. Work for three minutes.

649
Try Indian head massage

Stress can be detrimental to hair health, particularly when neck and shoulder tension prevents blood circulation from taking nutrients and oxygen to hair follicles. Book a session with a therapist specializing in Indian Head Massage, which advocates gentle compression, repetitive percussive movements, hair tugs and rotations of the scalp to relieve muscular tension. Finger pressure on energy points aims to free up subtle energy blockages and rebalance the chakra energy centres. Ask for self-help techniques to use when shampooing.

650
Circulation-boost scalp massage
When shampooing or conditioning, place your fingertips at your hairline behind your ears on each side. With fingers curled, firmly rotate the tips, feeling skin moving over bone. Work towards the back of your head, until the fingertips of both hands meet.

Place your little fingers at the top of your hairline, thumbs by your ears. Rotate your fingertips over the top of the head and down to the nape of the neck.

Place your fingertips at your hairline at the nape of your neck. Make firm circular rotations, working up the hairline to finish behind the ears. Finally, circle your index fingers around your temples.

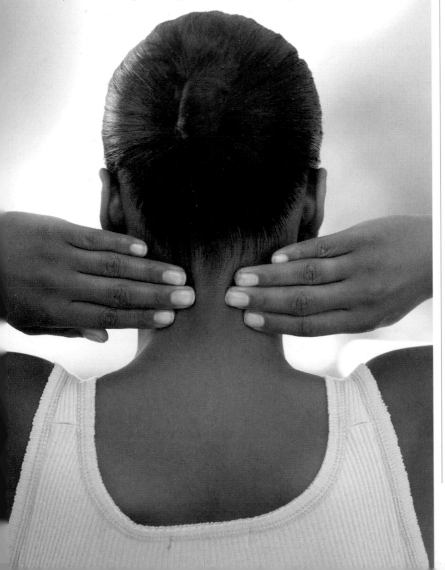

651
Eat your hair fitter
Make sure you are getting adequate B vitamins for hair health by adding eggs and whole grains, nuts, seeds and molasses to your diet. The B vitamins 3, 5 and 6 are essential for radiance; B$_2$ for repairs. Levels of the mineral silica, which strengthens nails and teeth as well as hair, decrease with age. Good foods for hair health include fruit and vegetables, small oily fish, seaweed, olive oil, nuts and seeds. Drink nettle tea for body and shine.

652
Salad dressings
When the scalp feels rough add 1 tbsp a day of hemp oil to salad dressings to moisturize from the inside out.

653
Avoid harsh shampoos
Dandruff shampoos may contain fungicides and other ingredients that can exacerbate an already dry, irritated or sensitive scalp. Opt instead for a once-a-week oil treatment and circulation-enhancing massage.

Boost circulation by giving yourself an invigorating scalp massage.

Organic shampooing

When choosing natural shampoos, don't worry if they don't foam: mild surfactants that don't irritate the scalp or pollute the marine environment don't seem to lather as exuberantly as chemical detergents. Don't be tempted to use more product than is recommended just because you are accustomed to more bubbles.

Choose natural shampoos that don't strip the scalp's protective lipid barrier.

654
Off-the-shelf products

Look for mild cleansers with botanical ingredients that protect hair from fallout and breakage. Burt's Bees Super Shiny Grapefruit and Sugar Beet Shampoo and Conditioner use marula oil to soften the scalp and add shine. Jurlique's Sandalwood Shampoo and Herbal Protein Conditioner suit brittle hair and dry scalps.

655
Don't mix products

If you mix conventional products not intended to be used together you risk setting up chemical reactions that lead to the production of potentially carcinogenic nitrosamines. Avoid products containing DEA and TEA (di- and triethanolamines) to cut out the risk.

656
Encourage hair growth

Add 1 drop each essential oils of lavender and rosemary to 1 tbsp shampoo before application. (Omit rosemary oil if you have epilepsy.)

657
Herbal nourishment

Place a handful each of rosemary, sage, nettle and goosegrass (cleavers) leaves in a bowl and pour over hot water. When cool, pour over clean, wet hair and leave for 15 minutes. Rinse. These herbs can prevent dandruff, inhibit greying, soothe scalp soreness and reduce hair loss.

658
Tonic for fine hair

Add 1 drop essential oil of cedarwood to 1 tbsp shampoo before application as a tonic for the hair.

659
Tea tree treat

Add 1 drop essential oil of tea tree to 1 tbsp shampoo before application for its cleansing properties.

Nourish your hair with a rosemary rinse.

660

Stimulating the scalp

Before shampooing add 1 drop essential oil of geranium to 1 tbsp shampoo to stimulate blood flow to the scalp.

661

Rinse well

After shampooing you can't rinse hair enough. Using plenty of clean water and gradually taking the temperature as cold as you dare may be all that's needed to create shine.

662

Herbs for shine

Following the final rinse, pour a pot of cooled herbal tea over your hair: sage tea for shine; thyme or yarrow to encourage growth.

663

Vinegar restorer

To remove built-up hair product and restore the hair shaft's acid mantle after shampooing, add half a cup of cider vinegar to the final rinse water.

664

Natural perfuming

After semi-drying, scent hair by tousling over smoke from a stick or cone of sandalwood incense (avoid if using flammable styling products).

665

Thyroid care

Hair thinning might be a sign of an under-active thyroid gland. Ask your doctor to check it out. The Australian Bush Flower Essence Old Man Banksia helps rebalance the thyroid, or take a supplement of *Fucus vesiculosis* (a seaweed rich in iodine) and eat iodine-rich foods.

666

Homeopathic hair-loss remedies

- Fluor.Ac 30c helps when hair loss follows an acute illness, such as flu.
- Sepia 30c boosts growth when loss follows childbirth or the menopause.
- Weisbaden Aqua 30c is reputed to promote hair growth and darkening; take for at least a month.

Conditioning treatment

Once a week treat hair to a deep conditioning treatment with nourishing oils and masks that impart useful nutrients for hair and scalp health. For extra dry and brittle hair, use oil treatments twice a week until you see results.

667

Prewash mud mask for dry hair and scalp

Apply this treatment before relaxing in a warm bath.

1 strip dried seaweed
4 tbsp Dead Sea mud
1 tbsp runny honey
1 tbsp grapeseed oil
1 cup green tea, cooled
2 drops each essential oils of
    rosemary and cedarwood

In a large bowl, crumble the seaweed into the mud. Stir in the honey, oil and enough green tea to make a firm paste. Drop in the essential oils. Plaster over the scalp and dry hair.

Pile hair on top of the head, place a plastic bag over the scalp and wrap in warm towels. Relax for 20 minutes. Rinse and shampoo. (Omit rosemary oil if you have epilepsy.)

668

Warm oils

Warming oil allows it to penetrate the hair shaft better. Divide hair into sections, and apply evenly through each section, then blow hot air over the head for 5 minutes. Comb hair through, wrap in a towel and allow the oil to penetrate for 20 minutes before shampooing. Alternatively, apply the oil before using the sauna.

669

Overnight oiling

Argan oil is one of the best hair and scalp conditioners to leave on overnight. Smother onto dry hair and cover pillows with plenty of old towels before retiring. Or substitute olive, macadamia nut or rosehip oil.

670

Fragrant oil

Nourishing scented oils impart fragrance as well as gloss and swing.

2 tbsp extra-virgin olive oil
1 tbsp flaxseed oil
1 tbsp avocado oil
6 drops essential oil of sandalwood
5 drops essential oil of geranium
4 drops essential oil of jasmine

Mix the oils and massage into the scalp and hair. Wrap in a towel for one hour before shampooing.

671

Intense conditioner

Leave this conditioning oil on overnight for best results.

4 tbsp coconut oil
6 drops essential oil of rose
3 drops essential oil of ylang ylang

Mix oils and massage into the scalp and dry hair. Wrap in a warmed towel for 1 hour before shampooing. This also makes a powerfully scented serum to condition dry ends and tame curls. (Omit ylang ylang oil if you have an inflamed scalp or dermatitis.)

672

Dandruff scrub

Use this as a replacement for conventional anti-dandruff shampoos.

2 tbsp extra-virgin olive oil
1 tbsp runny honey
1 tbsp dried mint
1 tsp very finely ground black pepper
1 drop each essential oils of black
    pepper and peppermint

Mix together the oil and honey. Next, stir in the mint, pepper and the essential oils. Apply to dry hair and massage deeply into the scalp for 10 minutes, feeling the skin move over the underlying bone. Rinse well with warm water to get rid of any bits before shampooing.

673

Fresh hair mask

This age-old treat for the hair should be used with tepid water (hot water might lead to a curdled, scrambled egg effect).

- 1 egg yolk, beaten
- 3 tbsp natural yogurt
- 1 tsp avocado oil
- 4 drops essential oil of carrot seed

1 Combine the oils with the beaten egg and natural yogurt in a large bowl. Whisk until a smooth, runny paste is formed.

2 After shampooing, massage into wet hair from roots down. Rinse very well with cool, then tepid water. Finish with a blast of cold water.

Holistic hair colouring

Most of us notice grey hairs by the age of 40. Declining production of the pigment melanin by hair follicles as we age leads to loss of hair colour, especially among people with European heritage. By the age of 75 most of us are grey. Colouring hair is a popular response, but a number of ingredients in hair dyes may irritate sensitive skin.

Bright white hair looks stunning: dare to be different.

674
Going au naturel

If your tone of grey is an attractive one – bright white or dove grey, perhaps – consider flaunting it. Bright white hair looks especially stunning, and turns heads in age groups that usually colour.

675
Trust the professionals

If you choose to colour your hair, go to an experienced colour technician: she is more likely to achieve a natural-looking finish and to be able to suggest colour combinations and techniques that keep pace with youthful styling.

676
Patch testing

After the menopause skin sensitivity can become more acute. Even if you have been using one brand of hair dye for years, consider a patch test: place a tiny amount of dye on a small patch of skin 48 hours before treatment – try the inside of the wrist. If there is no reaction in the next 24 hours, go ahead and use the product. If you notice redness or itching, try another brand.

677
Choosing shades

It doesn't always work to return to the colour you were in your youth: if skin tone fades, this can look too harsh. An all-over tone can be unforgiving for a mature complexion. Opt for shades that are close to your skin colour (no more than two shades different). Ask a colour technician about a mix of high and lowlights, which blend more naturally into grey, brightening or warming its effect.

678
Colouring tips

If choosing to colour yourself, opt for semi-permanent dyes that fade over 12 weeks and don't leave obvious roots. Smear olive oil around your hairline and ears to avoid colouring your skin, then don protective gloves. Apply the colour with a brush from the roots down, working in sections.

679
Natural lowlights

Rinse through freshly washed hair for lowlights.

1 black tea bag
handful dried sage leaves
1 tbsp balsamic vinegar
2 drops essential oil of rosemary

In a large bowl pour 2 cups of boiling water over the tea bag and sage leaves. Infuse for 20 minutes. Stir in the vinegar and essential oil. Use as a final rinse after shampooing. (Omit rosemary oil if you have epilepsy.)

680

Red herbal highlights

Place a large handful each of marigold and camomile flowers in a pan and cover with water. Throw in 2 bags of hibiscus tea, then bring to a boil. Simmer for 10 minutes. Allow to cool then stir in 3 drops essential oil of rose and use as a final rinse.

681

Hair darkening oil

Mix 1 tsp walnut oil into overnight conditioning oil and work through the hair to bring out warm lowlights (do not use on very light hair).

682

Brightening rinse for fair hair

Use this combination as a final rinse after shampooing.

10 strands of saffron
1 bag camomile tea
juice of half a lemon

Place the saffron in a bowl with the tea bag and pour over 2 cups of boiling water. Leave to infuse for 20 minutes. Squeeze in lemon juice.

Hair removal

Although body hair growth slows as we age, the bad news is that it becomes coarser in texture and facial hair can become more noticeable in women. Waxes and depilatories may include ingredients irritating to dry skin and to varicose veins, while waxing can result in in-growing hairs. Here are some natural alternatives.

683

Threading

Although it works on the same principle as waxing, threading is less painful and less irritating to sensitive skin, since it doesn't involve use of hot wax (therapists pluck hairs with the aid of a twisted length of cotton). Indian women swear by weekly appointments for everything from eyebrows to legs.

684

Exfoliate before shaving

If the skin on your legs is prone to in-growing hairs, exfoliate before shaving, using an exfoliating scrub or brushing gently with a loofah. Go carefully over the delicate skin of the shins.

685

Post-shaving salve

Mix 3 drops essential oil of sandalwood into 1 tbsp hemp oil and massage in to soothe inflammation.

686

Olive oil lubrication

To soothe sensitive skin that reacts to soap and shaving foam or gel, rub olive oil into the skin 10 minutes before shaving. Apply just a little: too much clogs a razor. If you find olive oil too greasy, substitute a thin layer of aloe vera gel. This protects against nicks.

687

Anti-hair-growth mask

Indian women recommend twice-weekly overnight applications of this mask to reduce hair growth. Mix in enough rosewater to achieve a consistency you like.

1 tbsp rosewater
2 tbsp kaolin
3 drops essential oil of sandalwood

Stir the rosewater into the kaolin, then add enough warm water to make a smooth paste. Drop in the sandalwood oil. Apply to the areas where hair growth is a problem.

4 Health & wellbeing

Making four positive lifestyle changes really can maximize your chances of living long and well. They are to stop smoking, eat healthily, take exercise and drink moderately. Do all four and you cut the risk of dying prematurely by 65 per cent, according to one study. What else makes a difference as the years go by? Positive thinking, destressing and getting plenty of sleep all enhance wellbeing. In the end, however, the answer to eternal youth comes from locating an on-button within that keeps us alert, open to new experiences and engaged with the world around us – simply appreciating and enjoying life can go a long way towards extending it.

Stop smoking

Older people form the part of the population most likely to suffer from tobacco-induced disease and premature death: smoking shortens life by an average 12–15 years. Moreover, smoking is the second best way to age the skin (after UV exposure). According to the World Health Organization, tobacco is more addictive than heroin, cocaine, alcohol, caffeine and marijuana. Now is the time to stop!

688
Educate yourself
How much do you know about the risks of smoking as an older person? Studies suggest that you are unlikely to want to stop until you know the worst. Get online and find out now!

689
Never too late
Smoking for decades doesn't make it harder to give up – nor are the benefits reduced. Studies demonstrate that quitting even post 65 brings significant health benefits and extends lifespan. After five tobacco-free years, risk becomes close to that of a lifelong non-smoker.

690
Make a plan
The first step in quitting is to decide you want to stop (not just cut down). It may help to record your thinking in a journal. List reasons for quitting and explanations for why it hasn't worked in the past. Note alternative ways to cope with stressful events. Set down a date to aim for.

691
Nicotine replacement
Using appropriate nicotine replacement therapy, such as patches, gum, inhalers and nasal sprays or non-nicotine Zyban tablets, reduces cravings and withdrawal symptoms and can double your chance of quitting. Check with your doctor before buying off-the-shelf products.

692
Involve professionals
Consult your doctor about specialist clinics or groups that offer tailor-made quit-smoking programmes. For free advice in the UK call the NHS Stop Smoking Line (0800 1690 169) or Quitline (0800 02200).

693
Self-help groups
The camaraderie of other would-be non-smokers can help in the struggle to quit. Seek out a group local to home or work.

694
You need friends
Enlist the support of family, friends and work colleagues. Have them text you supportive messages and be there to help you resist temptation at difficult times. It's easiest to quit if a friend joins the struggle.

695
Avoidance strategies
It often helps to sever associations between smoking, socializing and alcohol. Save smoking for solitary sessions. Plan your social life around non-smoking friends and venues. Cut out alcohol during at least the first two months of quitting; this seems to boost willpower to keep up the good work.

696
Eat your greens
Make sure to eat cruciferous vegetables most days. Two daily helpings of broccoli, cauliflower or Brussels sprouts can reduce levels of tobacco toxins in smokers, claims the American Health Foundation.

Detox with cruciferous greens to get rid of tobacco toxins in your blood.

697

Detox with fruit and veg

Not only does smoking create free-radical molecules that prematurely age the body, smokers have lowered levels of the antioxidant vitamins needed to mop up the damage. As an antidote, pack your diet with free-radical-busting fruit and vegetables and drink plenty of water to flush away toxins.

698

Keep your fingers busy

When you just have to do something with your fingers, open pistachio nuts. They are a great snack for the heart, since they contain more cholesterol-lowering phytosterols than other nuts. Greek women swear by worry beads for occupying the hands. Knitting with chunky wool on large needles also brings satisfyingly speedy results.

699

Herbal help

To support and cleanse the lungs after giving up, take coltsfoot (*Tussilago farfara*) as a herbal tincture (30 drops daily in water) or as capsules (follow pack directions).

700

Try acupuncture

Researchers have found acupuncture effective in helping quit the habit. Ask your doctor about referral.

701

Homeopathic support

Take the remedy Caladium 30c daily for two weeks after giving up to modify cravings for tobacco. Take Nux.Vomica 30c daily for two weeks to help the body rid itself of nicotine. If you develop a cough after giving up as the lungs try to drain built-up catarrh, try a daily dose of Pulsatilla 30c until symptoms ease.

702

Apples help

Need to put something in your mouth? Try a crisp apple. The tangy freshness can stave off cravings.

703

Natural painkillers

Light, regular exercise reduces withdrawal symptoms and stimulates natural painkillers. Visit the gym when symptoms seem worse.

704

Deserving treats

Indulge in other pleasures: read a novel in a hammock, sunbathe for 15 minutes, have a few minutes extra in bed in the morning or enjoy dark chocolate after dinner.

705

Savings add up

An Ohio State University study demonstrated that for every year of smoking adults lost around 4 per cent of income. Put away the money you save by not smoking then buy something tangible: maybe a new sofa or a truly fabulous pair of shoes.

706

Keep trying

If you give in, don't feel a failure. Dust off your self-respect and start over. The average person takes seven goes to give up for life. Zero tolerance of tobacco is essential after giving up. Even after years of abstinence, just one ciggie can trigger cravings.

Destressing

We all need a little daily stress to motivate us to get up, and to provide the impetus to tackle challenges. But when stressors are psychological and frequent, and not enough time elapses for the body to recover from its stress responses, wellbeing suffers.

707
Get moving
A sure way to reduce stress levels is to take exercise. Aim for at least 30 minutes' activity a day. Fit people are more resilient to stress, require greater stimulus to invoke the stress response, and return to normal more quickly following stressful incidents.

708
Act like a woman
Women have ways of coping with stress that reduce negative health consequences. They use "tend and befriend" strategies while men tend to withdraw, act hostile or resort to drink or drugs. This may be why women outlive men by an average of seven and a half years.

709
Count your hours of sleep
On less than six hours' sleep, the brain seems to release stress hormones. During stressful periods, seek extra sleep in the form of daytime naps.

710
Relax in the bath
Soaking in warm water sedates the nervous system; effects are greater if you add a relaxing essential oil (see Nos. 579–97).

711
Learn to meditate
Meditation can return stress hormone levels to normal, relax muscles and slow a racing heart. If you can't achieve a daily practice, try to approach everyday activities in a state of mindfulness.

712
Herbs for stamina
Stress engages the "fight or flight" mechanism or adrenaline response; over time this exhausts the adrenal glands. The herb borage (*Borago officinalis*), traditionally given to soldiers before battle to engender courage, is a known adrenal stimulant. On a stressful day take 20–30 drops of the tincture in water to restore emotional stamina.

713
Try flower essences
Australian Bush Flower Essence combination Calm & Clear suits those who rush about trying to do

Borage, a known adrenal stimulant, is great for boosting emotional stamina.

Counter stress caused by sleep deprivation with an afternoon nap.

too much and consequently achieve little. It contains essences to aid concentration, calm a busy mind and promote mental focus.

714
Begin chanting

Chanting a mantra seems to help reduce stress, research reveals. Seek out a meditation class based on an Eastern tradition to learn how, or try Sivananda or Kundalini yoga, which teach the techniques.

715
Learn to pray

Sit or kneel comfortably upright. Adopt your regular prayer position with your hands. Close your eyes and focus on your breath.

On an out-breath repeat a prayer or holy word/s that have meaning for you. Repeat the invocation with every out-breath; let it melt away awareness of the body.

As you utter the holy words, bring them into your heart, giving up any thoughts or emotions you are holding on to. Let the holy word ignite the spark of divine within.

716
Keep a diary

If you've always got too much to do and too little time to finish everything, plan out your week in a diary. Build in space for leisure, relationships and down-time.

717
Ditch the overtime

People who work long hours are at increased risk of suffering injuries and sickness that trigger time off work. If you feel trapped in an overwork culture, might job-sharing, working part-time or freelancing be an option? If not, could you consider a career-switch, sabbatical or retraining?

718
Declare war on noise

Noise pollution – leaking iPods, tantrumming toddlers, wailing sirens – evokes an especially rapid stress response and women seem to have lowest tolerance levels. At home, turn off phones, TV and radio. Whenever possible, retreat to locations where wind and birdsong are the loudest audible events.

719
Attend a concert

Listening to live music can lower stress levels, reducing blood pressure and feelings of depression and anxiety, shows one study.

720

We need bread and roses

Build treats into difficult days. The heart needs constant nourishment from art and beauty, just as the body requires its daily bread. Spend lunchtime in a gallery, go to the ballet, place a bunch of organically grown roses on your desk.

721

Turn off the TV

Working long hours and watching TV are closely linked in studies. See how much less stressed you feel if you have non-TV evenings. Does this give you time to talk to your partner, finish chores, have a bath or simply go to bed earlier?

722

Keep a diary

Keep a stressors and triggers diary. Buy a notebook and rule each page into three columns. In the first column log each time you become angry. In the second column cite the stressor. In the third column write down what you could do, either by avoiding the stress factor or by reacting differently to it.

The beauty and scent of roses help you unwind and keep your baseline stress hormone levels low.

723

Tense and release

Lie on your back, arms and legs gently apart. Working from the toes up, tense every part of your body in turn, holding the tension before releasing on an out-breath. Include your feet, calves, thighs and buttocks, abdomen and chest, hands and arms, shoulders and neck, face and scalp. Feel how good relaxation is when compared with tension.

724

Productive jams

Make sure you always allow enough journey time. If you have to sit in traffic jams regularly, make them productive: learn a language from a CD, listen to audio books, lighten up with a radio comedy, or chill with a relaxation tape.

725

Bathe in white light

When everything is overwhelming, close your eyes and imagine a shower of bright white light beating down on the crown of your head. Feel it cleansing your body and washing away negative energy. Then imagine breathing in the pure white light, allowing it to seep into every organ and enter your bloodstream, bringing peace and purity. Finally, exhale the white light, letting it sit around your body like a force-field.

Beating anxiety

Ageing means change, whether as a result of emotional loss, physical ailments or mental decline. And for most of us, change brings anxiety. A Dutch study found that anxiety goes hand in hand with depression as we grow older, with women at greater risk than men. As anxiety can be a risk factor in many diseases, it pays to conquer it by adopting any natural approaches that work for you.

Burn essential oils with aromas that calm the mind and restore the spirit.

726
Prevent panic attacks
Take the homeopathic remedy Aconite 30c as soon as you start to feel panic rising to prevent it from developing. It is particularly helpful if you feel convinced you are about to die. Don't feel bad about this experience; it's more common than you might think!

727
Meditate on a thought
Think on the following quotation attributed to Mark Twain when anxiety strikes: "I'm an old man, and have known many troubles, but most of them have never happened."

728
Money troubles
If you tend to fret about financial security and spend hours studying bank statements and doing frantic calculations, take one dose of the homeopathic remedy Ars.Alb 30c, file bank statements away and go and do something enjoyable.

729
Knead putty
Buy yourself a few pots of silly putty – choose an outrageous colour. When you feel angry or can't keep a grip on an issue, knead out your tension or throw the putty against a wall. When you can't stand it any more, chuck the putty in the bin.

730
Saddle up
Try horseriding. Horses are thought to be highly responsive to human emotional states, and are increasingly used therapeutically. Practitioners suggest that spending time with horses heightens social relationships and promotes teamwork as well as fostering emotional growth.

731
Burn sandalwood oil
Place 8 drops of this meditation-enhancing essential oil in a room vaporizer to calm the mind and rejuvenate the nerves. Enjoy the balsamic woodiness of the scent.

732
Float away
To experience complete peace, try a session in a flotation tank, which guarantees the luxurious treat of total darkness, stillness and (if you choose one without whale music) complete silence. Note how much clarity you gain after a session.

733
Drink camomile tea
Camomile has a sedative, muscle-relaxant effect and works on the same part of the brain as anti-anxiety drugs. Steep teabags for at least 7 minutes, or use two bags per cup.

734
Connecting with the breath

When you feel flustered or restless, close your eyes and be aware of the flow of breath in and out. Feel it cool on your upper lip and warm in your nostrils. This calm space for retreat is always there, waiting for you to drop into it.

735
Driver shrug

At the wheel, lift your shoulders towards your ears. Squeeze tightly then drop on an exhalation. Repeat, then roll your shoulders up, back and down. Reverse the movement.

736
Bathing in green

Being surrounded by greenery can reduce nervous and muscular tension and promote calm positivity. If you commute to work through countryside, bathe in the different shades of green. In town, make diversions to spend daylight hours walking through parks.

737
Boost natural opiates

Boost circulation daily by going for a brisk walk or swim to pump freshly oxygenated blood around your body and fill your brain with natural opiates.

Use candle meditation to see the flame of life burning bright within.

738
Candle meditation

Light a candle and sit in front of it. When your body feels relaxed and your breathing is calm, begin to stare at the flame. Allow the light to erase thoughts from the present moment. Close your eyes and see your flame of life within. However brightly it's burning right now, give thanks. When you feel ready to blow out the candle, keep the thought of the flame within you burning bright.

739
Anxiety flower remedies

Try 7 drops morning and evening of the following Australian Bush Flower Essences:
• Dog Rose is good for a generally anxious nature, and particularly for anxiety about health.
• Crowea, for inveterate worriers who torment themselves with a thousand little negative "what ifs".
• Sturt Desert Rose, for those whose anxiety is mixed with guilt about having done the wrong thing.

740
Cry it out

If you feel like weeping, do: it sheds stress hormones and can make you feel pleasantly emptied and able to start again. Laughter is another natural healer.

741
Be good enough

It's enough to be a good-enough mother, boss, lover, employee or carer. Free yourself from having to achieve perfection all the time. When demands pile up and everyone expects, do what you can, keeping the perspective that in five years' time it probably won't matter.

742
Come back to the body

Lie on your back with legs stretched out, arms by your side. Close your eyes and visualize all the water within your body. Start to roll slowly onto one side, picturing liquid within each of your cells tipping almost imperceptibly. Continue to roll onto your front, trying not to jolt the water within. Keep rolling to the other side and onto your back again, taking as long as you need, so as not to upset the water. This exercise may take 20 minutes.

743
Spacious thinking
Close your eyes and look at what image appears when you say the words "empty mind". If it's a half-full cup, try to widen your perspective. Imagine sitting on a cliff top watching the horizon, following the line where sea and sky meet. When life feels confined, close your eyes and return to this spacious place.

744
Daydream downtime
Don't schedule every minute of the day for achieving stuff. Take time out while commuting, sitting at a desk or in the park to daydream, staring into space and going wherever your thoughts follow.

745
Lottery reverie
Have a million-dollar moment. Let your brain drift over all the things you'd do if you won the lottery. Travel, do good, live somewhere different. When you come to, ponder how you could make some of those wishes come true.

Lifting mood

Mood swings are a disconcerting but natural hazard of the menopausal years. To lessen highs and lows, cut back on caffeine and bag enough sleep: jittery nerves from sleep deprivation and copious coffee make down times seem worse. Try relaxation techniques – yoga and meditation are particularly helpful.

746
Skullcap tea
Many herbal formulas promise relief from depression, low mood, anxiety and insomnia. Skullcap (*Scutellaria lateriflora*) appears in almost all of them. Drink the tea or take 20–30 drops of the tincture daily in lots of water – it tastes very bitter.

747
Uplifting herbs
St John's wort (*Hypericum perforatum*) works well for many people with symptoms of depression because it acts as a monoamine oxidase inhibitor (the physiological mechanism used by the tricyclic class of antidepressant drugs). Consult a herbalist to find which form might suit you best – and take for at least two months. Consult your doctor if taking prescription drugs, including oral contraceptives, and avoid excessive exposure to sunlight.

748
Dealing with loss
If a low mood is a reaction to a loss or disappointment of some kind (a specific loss such as the death of a pet or a more general sense of disappointment about life), take the homeopathic remedy Ignatia 30c daily for short crisis periods. It is particularly suited to those prone to weeping or sighing.

Depression-beating
St John's wort works well if you are struggling with life's demands.

749
Burn oils
Add 3–4 drops of the following essential oils to a room vaporizer to lift mood: rose, jasmine, lavender, geranium, orange, frankincense.

750
Choose good fats
The brain requires oil to function well, particularly omega-3 fatty acids. Low concentrations have been linked with mood disorders, while good amounts enhance brain-cell receptors' ability to process and react to mood signals. Secure your fill from wild salmon and small oily fish, hemp, argan and flax (linseed) oils (rub onto the skin, too), grass-fed meat and organic cheese.

751
Plan to travel
Gaining perspective on life can be helpful when things seem difficult. One of the best ways to do this is to travel. Try a tour for like-minded people who enjoy art, rambling or ancient history, or a backpacking adventure that lifts you out of your own mechanical existence into the lives of others.

752
Become a poet
Writing poetry is recommended by some doctors as a way to wean patients from antidepressants. One study suggested writing poetry stimulated levels of immunoglobin A. If you find words hard to conjure up, buy a pack of poetry fridge magnets and enjoy composing a line or two when reaching for the milk.

753
Emotional relief with yoga
Yoga is supremely effective at calming an agitated mind. Try the pose below, or face a sofa, cross your legs and lean forwards resting your arms and head on the seat. Alternatively, see No. 361 for another restful pose.

1 Supta virasana: kneel about 30cm (1ft) away from a sofa with knees hip-width apart; try to place your bottom on the floor between your feet (pile cushions beneath your bottom until you are comfortable).

2 Lie back on the sofa with back and head completely supported (add pillows where necessary). Rest for 5 minutes, breathing gently. (Avoid this pose if you have varicose veins or phlebitis.)

754
Go for a run
You can feel better in just 30 minutes if you take exercise. Research on patients with a major depressive disorder demonstrated that a 30-minute workout at moderate intensity can disable anger, confusion, distress and fatigue associated with a bad mood.

755
Suffering can help!
Hardship may be important to some people in restoring equanimity. Climbing a mountain, walking a long trail, completing a journey by sail or oars can bring a sense of obstacles beaten, and a triumphing over self-obsession.

756
Get real
Don't try to be happy all the time: if you need to cry or rage, do so. Mood swings are part of life – and life can be unfair.

757
Visualizing confidence
Sit quietly and close your eyes. Think back to a time when you felt confident and optimistic. Perhaps after passing a driving test, a successful interview, getting married or giving birth. Recall how you felt. Fix this image by drawing an imaginary circle around your feet. Step out of the circle, knowing it's there whenever you need to step back in and psyche yourself up for a stressful event.

758
Start the day right
Make every morning a fresh start. Whatever happened yesterday, assert on waking that today will be filled with fresh possibilities. Vow to live in the present.

759
Seeking help
If dark moods affect your quality of life, get help before they start to affect your work and social life. This will make independence more likely into old age.

760
Plant bulbs
If you suffer from SAD (Seasonal Affective Disorder), anything that lifts the dreariness of the year's dark months can be helpful. In late summer plant bulbs to poke through the cold dark earth at that down time of year. Snowdrops, hyacinth and crocuses provide earliest colour. See them as a harbinger of spring warmth and new beginnings: new life needs a period of cold and dark in which to prepare to bloom.

Cook something really healthy to promote feelings of positivity.

761
Cook something good
Invest feelings of positivity in a dish to serve to others or for yourself. As you chop, fry and stir, mix in a little passion and personality by tuning into the scents, texture and taste and staying in the moment.

762
When you overeat
If, when you feel down, you need to eat carbohydrates, try adding sources of the mineral chromium to your diet – research suggests this may help when carb cravings typify depression. Sources include whole grains, green beans and broccoli.

763
Light matters
Try eating, reading or watching TV by daylight lightbulbs if lack of natural light gets you down in winter. Full-spectrum lightboxes, or even a light visor worn like a hat, offer more intense light therapy, although 30 minutes' daily exposure to real outdoor light is best.

764
Drink lemon balm tea
Try lemon balm tea, which is known to reduce anxiety, for its calming qualities. (Avoid in pregnancy.)

765
No-technology day
A survey of 1500 men and women found that the more time they spent at a computer, the more depressed they were likely to be. If technology overload is causing you to feel stressed or affects performance and decision-making, set limits for time spent online, telephone rather than email and set aside time for socializing and destressing. Have one technology-free day a week.

766
Quick fix flowers
Bach Flowers Rescue Remedy is a must for destressing in situations of shock or when you need instant

results. Place 4 drops in a glass of water and sip until symptoms subside. In extreme cases place the four drops direct on the tongue.

767
Embrace your rage
Give vent to feelings of anger in a positive way and you are less likely to suffer from depression and anxiety, studies suggest. Holding in emotions may increase levels of stress hormones in the body. Use anger as a tool for positive change in life or relationships, and address the issues that cause it. When you're over the outrage, express the depth of your feelings honestly, and state what needs to change, listing the consequences if nothing does.

768
Write a letter
If a death has brought about unresolved issues or regrets, write a letter or an email to the deceased. If it helps post it in a post-box or send it into cyberspace.

Positive thinking

Optimists live healthier, more fulfilled lives than pessimists. They also live longer than people who see their glass as half empty. But modern, busy lives seem to mitigate against contentment: we are perhaps too bombarded by demands to appreciate the happiness of the present moment.

769
Flower power for optimism
The best Flower Essence to promote optimism is the Australian Bush Flower remedy Sunshine Wattle. It is a good choice for people who take a grim view of the future because past events have been difficult. Take 7 drops morning and evening for two weeks. Chrysanthemum from the Flower Essence Society range supports those having difficulty accepting ageing. Place 2 drops in a glass of water and sip four times a day, or as necessary.

770
Laughter benefits
Laughing helps blood circulate more effectively. Increased blood flow means more oxygen and nutrients where they need to be. Hit a comedy club or watch reruns of comedy classics on TV.

771

Manage anger

Anger increases risk of suffering an injury or accident, suggests research. It is also a risk factor in reduced immunity, stroke, heart and circulation problems. If you are prone to anger enrol on an anger-management course and keep a diary listing triggers, reactions and remedies.

772

Look in on yourself

Try to see yourself from the perspective of someone looking in on your life. Refer to yourself in the third person. Does she enjoy life to the full? Does he make the most of opportunities? Why does she spend so much time frowning?

773

Challenge your inner voice

If you have a demon on your shoulder constantly berating you or telling you that you've blown it, magic him into a guardian angel who instead brings you more rational and empowering words.

774

Ditch negative stereotypes

If you regard growing older as becoming decrepit, uninteresting and depressed, you are more likely to age prematurely. Indeed, one study found those who had such negative perceptions experienced hearing decline earlier than those who saw ageing as a golden time of positive possibilities.

775

Smile at strangers

Dare to give a stranger a smile, even if you don't feel full of the joys of spring. Studies suggest even pretending to be happy makes us feel joyful and spreading love makes the world a more positive place for everyone.

Shed inhibitions and play games with your children or grandchildren.

776

Just play

Find excuses to lose your inhibitions and play: try tag or dressing up with grandchildren, organize softball or cricket on the beach, throw a Frisbee in the park, hold a Scrabble party with neighbours.

Stunning stilettos: sashay forth in high heels to feel empowered and sexy.

777
Learn to walk in heels

For many women wearing high heels is empowering, sexy and life-affirming. If you find it hard, practise at home, leading movement from the hips and keeping the shoulders back. Alternatively, opt for wedges.

778
Spend time outdoors

Natural light increases serotonin in the brain for instant positivity and stress-reduction. Spend a little time often in the sun, aiming for 10–15 minutes' sunbathing without sunscreen before 11am or after 3pm.

779
Count your blessings

At the end of every day think on the good things that happened. On bad days look for silver linings. (The gearbox went? At least it didn't happen on the motorway. Your heel snapped? Time for a shopping trip.) Give thanks for blessings daily.

780
Thought affirmations

Hang on to these thoughts: "I can do anything I choose", "Today I'll eat well and exercise", "I'm glad I've reached this age; I now have confidence and experience".

781
Treat yourself

Knock off early when there's good swell if you're a surfer; spend a day clothes' shopping at the start of the season; catch the matinee of a new show. Pleasure is wrinkle-lightening.

782
Savour life

Contemplating death forms part of the world's great religions for a reason: it makes us more positive about living life to the full. One lunchtime, spend time perusing gravestones or sitting in a churchyard in quiet contemplation of the transitory nature of human existence. Before you leave, vow to do something that enhances your life and the lives of those you love.

Life-affirming sex

Feeling sexy is essential if we are to maintain a sense of self-worth and body confidence while nature does its best to wrinkle the skin, send the breasts south and dry up essential juices. Regular sexual activity provides more than a full-body workout and is a sure way to cement a happy partnership; it can relieve insomnia, stress headaches and back pain according to research studies, in part by stimulating the release of natural opiates – stress-fighting endorphins.

783
Be glad you're over 40
Heed the wisdom of the chief executive of Coco de Mer, the high-end erotic fantasy emporium, who states that it is women over 40 who are leading the new sexual revolution. Women in their 30s are too all-consumed by babies; those in their 20s are working all hours to step onto the property and career ladders, while those in their teens are too scared to enjoy good sex. That leaves us having it all.

784
Be daring
Ditch your greying underwear and sensible nightie for something a little more thrilling. Even if you're not ready for nipple tassels or pubic jewels, track down some lace, lacings or leather on websites such as www.coco-de-mer.co.uk or www.agentprovocateur.com. Use low lights and scents to make your boudoir more sensual and explore tools for the bedroom arts.

785
Close your eyes
If you feel inhibited by your ageing body, close your eyes and rely on the truth of your inner eye, which works by feel and imagination, not looks. The inner you is whatever age you want her to be.

786
Watch a burlesque show
Try to catch a show by a feathered and diamond-encrusted showgirl – take a bunch of girlfriends. Artistes such as the corseted and curvaceous Dita Von Teese and Immodesty Blaize (who does a saucy reverse striptease) are reclaiming womanly erotica from porn-star raunch culture. Be inspired to try a cheeky umbrella dance at home.

787
Turn on your brain
Try some erotic fiction written by women for women to turn on the body's most erotic organ, the brain. Erotica is a growth category in women's romantic fiction; look for books by the imprints Ellora's Cave, Red Sage Publishers, Avon Red or Harlequin Spice.

788
Write IOU notes
Reward a lover for good behaviour with an IOU note for a French kiss, weekend away or passion in the back seat of the car.

789
Write erotic poetry
If you find love poetry embarrassing, take some mundane, everyday writing for inspiration – your computer manual is a safe place to start. Open at random and using only the words on that page compose an erotic verse. Have fun with terms such as "hard", "drive" and "input".

790
Love yourself
Make a list of your positive points – think beyond your physical assets, to your personal qualities or achievements. Read it regularly and keep adding to it. Encourage a

Plan time with your partner – don't underestimate the importance of talking.

partner to add his or her perceptions. Compose an affirmation based on your positive attributes to repeat on waking daily.

791
Plan special time together

Take it in turns to arrange special events for one another (especially if it's you that usually organizes your social life as a couple). Relinquishing control can enhance feelings of spontaneity. Whatever you do, make sure that two or three evenings a week you turn off the TV and just talk.

792
Aphrodisiac bath oil

Run a bath for two. Pour into it this sensual oil then relax and enjoy the aphrodisiac effect.

1 tbsp sweet almond oil
4 drops essential oil of rose
2 drops each essential oils of jasmine
   and myrrh

Mix the oils together, then swish into the bath just before you both are ready to step in. Scatter rose petals or jasmine flowers over the surface to make the bath even more romantic.

793
Scent pillows

The mind forms strong bonds between scent and experience. Perfume pillows with a few drops of essential oil of lavender or natural vanilla extract so the scent lingers on your hair and that of your lover. Whenever he catches a whiff during the day he will be reminded of you.

794
Sensual massage oil blend

Each of the essential oils in this sensual massage blend has aphrodisiac properties.

4 tbsp grapeseed oil
12 drops essential oil of jasmine
6 drops essential oil of sandalwood
4 drops essential oil of ylang ylang

Pour the grapeseed oil into a clean, dark glass bottle. Drop in the essential oils, lid and store in a cool, dark place. Shake well before use.

795
Valuing touch

People who are touched regularly heal more quickly and stay healthy for longer according to studies of people with HIV. If you're not in a physical relationship right now, book a full-body massage once a month to nurture your need for loving touch, and think about acquiring a cat to stroke.

796

Tantric temptation

Book a Tantra weekend with a lover. Don't be scared: it will give you space to think about your connection to each other in a more spiritual way and help you confront insecurities. And you're sure to meet interesting couples.

797

Get fishy

Fish, seafood and sea vegetables, such as seaweed and samphire, contain levels of minerals and vitamins including zinc, vitamin E and amino acids that are essential for healthy sex organs. Tempt with oysters and sushi.

798

Aphrodisiac ingredients

Eating should be a sensual delight. Crank it up with ingredients thought to have aphrodisiac qualities since ancient times:
- Pomegranate seeds are suggestive of fecundity.
- Fresh figs, broken open, can be eaten suggestively.
- Avocado is said to recall testicles.
- Red berries are thought to resemble nipples.
- Cream can be used for dipping berries.
- Honey, drizzled, is a cure for impotence.
- Rocket, coriander and basil give sexy bite.
- Aniseed: suck the seeds and increase desire.
- Asparagus is the perfect shape to nibble.
- Oysters are suggestive seafood.
- Almonds and marzipan are great for arousing female passion.
- Dark chocolate stimulates the brain.
- Espresso coffee will keep you perked up.

799

Take the initiative

Slip your mobile number to someone who takes your fancy as you alight from the bus or train.

800

Partner breathing

Lie close to each other (the spoons position is ideal). Close your eyes and listen to each other's breathing. **Gradually change** your breathing pattern to match your partner's flow of breath in and out. Swap, so that he or she follows your breath.

Once you are really relaxed, start to exchange breath. As your partner finishes breathing out, start your exhalation. At the end of your exhalation he or she starts to inhale. Repeat as long as it feels good.

801

Take flowers

If difficult past sexual experiences have left you feeling unsure of yourself sexually, try 7 drops twice daily of the following Australian Bush Flower Essences:
- Wisteria helps women resolve negative beliefs or expectations about sex.
- Flannel Flower promotes sensitivity and gentleness in men who have learned to repress their emotions.

Make eating a sensual experience with aphrodisiac foods such as fresh ripe figs.

A good night's sleep

While we sleep, organs, bones and tissue repair, and emotions and memories shift from an active to a storage part of the brain, essential for long-term memory. Insomnia is a common concern in later life, especially for women. What keeps us awake? Worry and health problems, according to a telephone survey of 1,000 Americans. And hot flushes.

802
How much do you need?
Some people do well on five hours' sleep; others need nine. If you suffer from insomnia and go to bed out of habit rather than tiredness, it may be time to rethink your routine. See what happens if you go to bed an hour later, or if you rise earlier.

803
Natural rhythms
While on holiday learn about how much sleep you need by going to bed when you feel tired and getting up when you wake naturally. See how it pans out over a week or longer, and reflect on how winter and summer bedtimes and waking times vary.

804
Don't take problems to bed
Women are more likely than men to lie in bed worrying. Keep a notebook by the bed to jot down concerns or things you just have to remember, then let them go. If you stay up late finishing chores, make a weekly rota to distribute tasks or cut back to essentials only.

805
Scheduling sleep
If you crave an extra hour's sleep, but can't fit it into a busy working life, add time incrementally by hitting the sack just 15 minutes earlier. After a week add another 15 minutes. Repeat until a month later you retire one whole hour earlier.

806
Eat before bed
Tryptophan is an amino acid that helps reduce anxiety and elevate serotonin, a brain chemical that promotes relaxation. In a recent study, mild insomniacs who ate a tryptophan-rich snack before bed reported more restful sleep and enhanced alertness next morning. Try a small chicken, tuna or egg sandwich on wholemeal bread (carbs promote sleepiness), a banana, glass of milk, oat cake or handful of almonds or sunflower seeds.

807
Try visualization
Rather than counting sheep, put yourself in a peaceful place. Imagine lying in warm sand on a balmy beach, reclining beside a tumbling waterfall or watching a golden sunset. Experience the scene with all your senses: what can you hear, feel and smell? In research studies at Oxford University, insomniacs who visualized themselves in a relaxing scene found sleep 20 minutes sooner than usual.

808
Stop obsessing
Aim to think flexibly rather than obsessing about a sleep "problem". Two hours' lost sleep a night doesn't reduce the ability to perform tasks states the UK's leading sleep expert, Professor Jim Horne.

809
Sleep thinner
If you need a prompt to retire early, write this on a sticky note: "Lack of sleep may make me fat". Research at Columbia University Medical Centre found that people who got less than five hours' sleep a night were 50 per cent more likely to be

obese than those who slept for eight hours. Lack of sleep equates with raised production of an appetite-stimulant hormone, and a reduction in a hormone that promotes the feeling of being sated.

810
Establish a routine
Decide on a sensible bedtime, then write a timed plan of how you can achieve it. It might go like this: turn off computer, eat, wash up, take a warm bath, read or listen to music, turn off the light. Set real times to each activity, and stick to them.

811
Creating a love temple
Remove all work-associated items from your bedroom. Devote the room to sleep (and love-making) only, and make up your bed weekly with crisp, clean linen.

812
Restful lavender oil
Store lavender bags between bed linen and put 5 drops of essential oil of lavender on your pillow.

813
Keep to schedule
Condition body and mind to expect sleep by getting up and going to bed at the same time every day, even

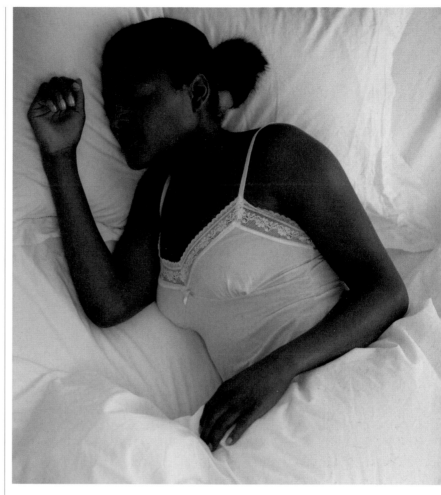

Getting a good night's sleep keeps the body functioning well and skin looking good.

when last night was a bad one. Try not to veer more than an hour or so away from routine at weekends.

814
Invest in blackout blinds
Find curtains that block every chink of light from a bedroom. Close doors and unplug nightlights. The less light in a room, the less the body is prompted to release the

adrenaline-like hormone cortisol, which prevents easy sleep. To help you down, spend evenings by candlelight.

815
Limit caffeine
If you have trouble sleeping, limit yourself to two small cups of coffee a day and enjoy them in the morning: the body can take 12 hours

to clear caffeine. After noon avoid coffee, black tea, drinking chocolate and soft drinks.

816

Relax before bedtime

Don't do worrying things just before you go to bed – sorting finances and paying bills, planning a wedding, arguing with teenagers, watching a documentary about child labour are all anxiety inducers. Opt for a little light cross-stitch or an erotic novel instead.

817

Power napping

Embrace the afternoon slump in energy levels: it's a perfectly natural dip and is the body/mind's way of making it through a long day. If you can, take a 15-minute nap – this is the best reviver there is.

818

Top homeopathic insomnia remedies

During a spell of insomnia, take up to three times daily. Stop when you start to feel better or after a week if it has not helped:
- Arg.Nit 30c may help break a cycle of sleeplessness maintained by a sense of anxiety ("What if I can't sleep?") as bedtime approaches.
- Ars.Alb.30c is for very restless people who must get up and pace about or tidy when they can't sleep.
- Coffea 30c is for when sleeplessness is a result of excitement or an over-active mind.

819

Herbal companions

Look for the herbal combination valerian, passiflora and scutellaria to promote restful sleep. All are

Dried rose petals, mint and cloves make a fragrant herbal sleeping bag.

available as teas or can be used in capsule form for a stronger effect (take as directed on the pack). Valerian is a mild tranquillizer but, unlike the drug derived from it, is not addictive. (Avoid if pregnant or taking conventional sleeping medication.)

820

Make a soothing herbal sleeping bag

Follow a recipe from 1606 by placing a couple of handfuls of dried rose petals and 1 tbsp each dried mint and cloves in the centre of a piece of muslin. Tie the corners together to secure, then place beneath your pillow.

821

Exercise in the morning

If you have problems going to sleep, don't exercise within three hours of bedtime. Instead take a morning walk in sunshine: bright light stimulates the production of melatonin which ensures daytime alertness and night-time drowsiness.

822

Rearrange your diary

If you're not someone who springs into action the moment your lids lift, try not to arrange early morning appointments. Slow brain function can last a full two

Soak in warm water before you go to bed to soothe body and mind.

825

Practise restful yoga

In a study by Harvard Medical School women slept more than half an hour longer following 10 weeks of bedtime yoga that focused on meditation and breathing. Follow the instructions for the resting supported bridge pose (see No. 956) by raising your hips on yoga blocks as you let the whole body relax for a better night's sleep.

826

Don't just lie there

If you have trouble dropping off or wake regularly during the night, don't lie in bed for more than 20 minutes. This can send stress levels soaring and fix associations between bed and lack of sleep. Instead, get up, leave the room, sip camomile tea and read a dull book. As soon as your eyelids start to droop, head back to bed again.

hours after waking, hindering performance and decision-making, according to a recent report in an American medical journal.

823

Take a warm bath

Have a warm bath before bed to soothe body and mind: add 10 drops essential oil of lavender mixed into 1 tsp sweet almond oil, or 12 tbsp Dead Sea salts.

824

Excess weight insomnia

Sleep apnoea may affect those who are overweight (untreated, it raises the risk of high blood pressure, heart attack, stroke and liver damage). If you have symptoms such as daytime tiredness, snoring, night-time breathing issues and morning headaches, go and see your doctor.

Community spirit

People who surround themselves with a community of friends, family and neighbours tend to live longer. Establishing good bonds with those around us promotes a healthy state of mind, which results in enhanced immunity and reduced risk of heart and circulatory problems.

827

Don't worry if you hate them

If your circle of family and friends is riven with squabbles and rivalry, you will win in the mental sharpness stakes according to one US study. Be thankful to your difficult acquaintances for that at least!

828

Make friends online

Thanks to the internet, we can widen our circle of friends and support networks to encompass the globe. Join chatrooms and converse on message boards with people who share your interests.

829

Use support groups

Having an online support community has been found to be especially positive for older people with chronic health conditions. In one study, 74 per cent of people who took part in an online diabetes group felt more hopeful about their condition after online discussions. Let this be your stimulus to sign up.

830

Flower power

Try these Bach Flower Essences if you find socializing difficult:
- Beech helps if you tend to be critical of others and avoid people because you feel irritated by them.
- Water Violet is for self-reliant and private people who find it hard to come out of their shell.

831

Join a craft circle

Keeping the brain engaged and creative juices flowing may be one of the keys to longevity and retaining brainpower. If knitting by the fire seems too tame for you, look out for guerrilla knitters, stitch 'n' bitch groups, and macramé and mojito nights.

832

Don't retire early

Resist the urge to give up your job just yet. People who work beyond the age of 55 seem to live longer than those who retire early, according to a study reported in the *British Medical Journal* – this may be because working maintains camaraderie, social relationships and a sense of purpose.

Enhance longevity by joining a knitting circle. It keeps the brain engaged and encourages social interaction.

833

Eat locally

Not only do you benefit the countryside if you "eat your view", spending on local food keeps money in your community.

834

Photo therapy

Research suggests we gain in positivity from simply looking at photographs of loved ones.

835

Make friends in faith

If your friendship group is faith-based, add points to your youthful quotient: one study found attending religious services lowered anxiety and stress, adding seven years to life.

836

Volunteer today

Giving up precious time to do something kind or helpful to others advances longevity, studies reveal.

837

Talk to someone new

Once a week start a conversation with someone you usually ignore – the checkout girl or the bus driver. Think about how it enhances life.

Detoxing

Good health depends upon the liver, the body's main organ of detoxification. But liver function declines with age: size and blood flow decrease and the organ finds it harder to metabolize (or process) toxic substances and withstand stress. Since so many body systems rely on the liver, take time to nurture it (and to look after the body's other organs of detoxification: the skin, kidneys, colon and lungs). Care is especially welcome after a period of over-indulgence.

Detox your system with plenty of water.

838
Herbal cleansing
Dandelion and burdock make a good general detox combination. Use 30 drops of the tincture in water or take capsules, following dosage advice on the pack. Burdock cleanses the digestive system, and dandelion promotes bile flow and is a great liver tonic.

839
After illness
For detoxing after taking antibiotics, take homeopathic remedies Sulphur 30c in the mornings and Nux.Vomica 30c in the evenings for a week.

840
Detox with the seasons
In spring and autumn, cleanse the liver with the herb milk thistle (*Carduus marianus*), which encourages liver cell renewal and

repair. Take 30 drops of the tincture in water daily, or take capsules as directed for a month or so.

841
Weekend nurture
After a period of excess spend a weekend nurturing body and mind. Eat three light meals daily based on plant foods and fish (stop eating before you feel full) and keep well hydrated. Rest (turn off electronic equipment) and focus on destressing activities, such as yoga or meditation.

842
Nuke a hangover
Homeopathic remedy Nux.Vomica 30c is a fantastic hangover cure. It has a particular affinity for the liver, stimulating it to process toxins quickly, so much so it has been known to encourage bad habits (as in "what the hell, I can always take Nux.Vomica in the morning!").

843
Eat and drink well
Build your detox regime around antioxidant fruit and vegetables, whole grains, fish, nuts and seeds and natural yogurt. Drink at least eight glasses of water daily, supplemented with peppermint, fennel and camomile teas.

844
Encourage circulation
A daily walk encourages circulation and lymph drainage, which is also helped by drinking lots of water.

845
Balancing fluids
If drinking more water makes you pee more, your kidneys, which are largely responsible for fluid balance, may benefit from a few drops daily (in water) of a tincture of the herb barberry (*Berberis vulgaris*).

846

Lengthening the breath

To rid yourself of toxic emotions, close your eyes and focus on your breath moving in and out. As you relax, notice how your out-breath lengthens naturally. Try to lengthen the out-breath so it is double the length of the in-breath. Imagine exhaling negative emotions as you lengthen the out-breath.

847

Passive twisting

Lie on your back with your knees bent and feet flat on the floor. Take your arms out at shoulder height, palms up. On an exhalation let the knees drop smoothly to the floor on one side and allow them to rest. Take five easy breaths. Inhaling, lift your knees back to the starting position. On an exhalation, drop your knees to the other side and rest, as before.

848

Joint circling

To open the body's energy gates at the start of your detox regime, follow this warm-up sequence. Start each movement small, then make the action more expansive. Enjoy the feeling of everything moving and shake out each body part afterwards.

1 Take a stance with feet hip-width apart. Raise one foot a little and rotate the ankle clockwise, then anti-clockwise. Repeat on the other ankle.

2 Place your hands on your hips and make circles with your pelvis. Move your hands to your knees and make circles in both directions.

3 Now extend one arm fully, as if trying to grow it. Rotate the arm, describing the biggest circle in the air you can. Repeat with the other arm.

849

Passive backbend

Roll up a blanket and place it on the floor. Lie on your back with the blanket level with where a bra strap would be, under the lower part of the shoulder blades. Spread out your arms at shoulder height, palms up. Lie in position, breathing, softening your chest and spine.

850

... and relax

After exercising, rest in yoga's supine relaxation pose (see No. 361). This allows the body time for recovery, supporting detoxification.

851

Dry brushing

Before a shower or bath dry-brush the skin with a loofah or body brush, making long strokes in the direction of the heart. This boosts circulation and sweeps away dead skin cells. It also acts as something of an antidote to a sedentary lifestyle.

852

Clean-air plants

Studies at Oslo University found increasing the number of indoor plants in a room reduced headaches and improved concentration. Try the common peace lily, spider plant and Boston fern. English ivy is recommended as an indoor cleanser to help people with allergies breathe more easily.

853

Smoke-free home

Toxins from tobacco smoke include the same carbon dioxide as emitted from car exhausts, tars, cyanide, arsenic and some of the dangerous ingredients found in floor cleaners, paint stripper, industrial solvents and rocket fuel. These toxins gather in dust, carpets and soft furnishings. Stop smoking to detox your home.

854

Organic only

When detoxing, eat only organic produce to avoid introducing more toxins into your system. This is especially important when consuming fats and animal products.

855

Lemon kickstart

Kickstart liver-cleansing by drinking the juice of a freshly squeezed lemon in water every morning before eating or drinking.

856

Press the great eliminator

To tone the digestive system and ease head pain, exert firm, circling pressure with the thumb of one hand onto the back of the other, where the base of the thumb and index finger meet. Keep up the pressure for 30 seconds. Repeat on the other hand. Avoid when pregnant.

857

Forgiving with flowers

For emotional detoxing, the best forgiveness flower essence is Dagger Hakea from the Australian Bush Flower range.

858

Sort out your junk

Hoarders can find themselves holding onto a lifetime's negativity in the form of clothes that no longer fit, incomplete work or studies, treatments for old illnesses, and out-of-date foods. Once a year, detox problem areas: beneath the bed and under the stairs, medicine and filing cabinets and your kitchen cupboards.

859

Explore journaling

When life seems to hit a crossroads, try a journaling exercise. Without thinking too hard or for too long, write about what you want to take into the next phase of your life and list the things you need to leave behind. It might be people, emotions, ways of coping with stress, work or lifestyle habits. Set aside an hour or so for the exercise.

Healthy heart

Age brings increased susceptibility to cardiovascular disease – one of the greatest risk factors simply being over 65. Reducing risk is relatively simple: stop smoking, eat healthily and be active most days. Happily, what's good for the heart keeps the brain acting youthfully, too.

860

Assess your risk

Get to know the risk factors for cardiovascular disease for people over 50: smoking, high blood pressure or cholesterol, diabetes and obesity. If you tick yes to two or more, you are 50-69 per cent more likely to develop the disease suggests a study published in one medical journal. Visit your doctor to work out ways to reduce your risk.

861

Quit smoking

Smokers are up to five times more likely to have a heart attack earlier in life than non-smokers. Twenty a day doubles your risk of developing heart disease. Try the stop-smoking ideas in Nos. 688–706.

862

Sleep well

A study of people aged 32–59 suggested sleeping five hours or less a night might increase risk of high blood pressure. Aim for seven or eight hours to allow the heart to slow and blood pressure to drop.

863

Destress

Stress can raise blood pressure and release stress hormones detrimental to heart health. Use all the destressing techniques that work for you (see Nos. 707–25) to reduce daily niggles. Establish a long-term stress-reduction plan by enrolling on a term's meditation, t'ai chi or yoga course. Alternatively, book a session with a life coach.

864

Herbal support

Drinking herbal tea is an easy way to support the heart as you grow older. Try hawthorn (*Crataegus oxyacantha*) tea bags. This herb is widely used as a cardiac tonic and circulatory stimulant. Studies have shown that it improves coronary circulation, reducing risk of angina and helping normalize blood pressure.

865

Giving and receiving

This breathing exercise stretches the subtle energy pathway known as the heart meridian, opens the chest, and reminds you that love is about giving and receiving. Stand with feet hip-width apart and arms crossed over your chest (hugging yourself), head down. Inhaling, open your arms and chest as wide as possible, raising your head. Exhaling, close your arms gently around yourself. Repeat several times, changing the cross of your arms each time.

866

Take up saunas

If you don't have a heart condition, start taking weekly saunas, shown in Japanese studies to reduce risk of heart problems in susceptible men.

867

Just chill

Those who are quick to anger may be more at risk of heart attack, angina, heart failure or stroke. Feeling angry in middle age makes you more than twice as likely to suffer heart disease and heart attacks later in life than if you maintain a calm disposition. Adopt strategies that stop you reacting with hostility to stressful situations or people: counting to 10, taking a deep breath, texting a friend or lunchtime kick-boxing sessions.

868

Speak out

In one study, male civil servants aged from 35–55 who felt justly treated at work had less risk of coronary heart disease than those who felt badly treated. If you sense injustice at work, try to resolve issues not by moaning to colleagues, but by speaking out to those who have the power to help: managers, personnel, union reps.

869

Keep the faith

If you have spiritual faith your blood pressure is likely to stay low, regardless of your age and size, found researchers at a university medical centre in North Carolina.

870

Acquire a dog

Dog owners are less likely to succumb to heart disease, and heal more speedily from illness and surgery, research suggests. Enjoy the companionship and enforced walks.

871

Take exercise

The hearts of people who exercise show fewer signs of ageing. Regular exercise reduces risk of heart attack and stroke, lowers blood pressure and raises levels of healthy

cholesterol. T'ai chi benefits heart health, too, found researchers from Tufts University Medical School, Boston. Improvements in heart health can be measured just three months after starting a programme.

872

Start walking

If you hate getting sweaty, be reassured by research suggesting that walking can be as effective in

Exercise the heart to combat the effects of ageing.

reducing cardiovascular problems as more vigorous workouts. Walking two miles a day reduces heart attack risk by almost a third. Aim to walk briskly for at least 2½ hours a week. In a study reported in a US medical journal, women who did so gained as many benefits as those who devoted the same amount of time to more aerobic forms of exercise.

873

Look after your teeth

People with gum disease seem to be at higher risk of heart attack according to studies, regardless of their age, weight or cholesterol level. Use the essential toothcare tips in Nos. 559–78.

874

Find 10 minutes

If you don't have time for a full exercise regime, just do 10 minutes – this brings health benefits, though not the full complement of a full-on 30-minute daily training session.

875

Work those calves

Calf exercise acts like invisible support hose, sending blood back to the heart and so relieving (and preventing) varicose veins. Find hills to walk up and perform calf lifts when standing in queues. At your desk flex and extend your feet and, keeping your heels down, lift

and lower your toes. Spend time daily with feet raised above your head (resting against a wall or sofa).

876

Eat whole grains

Older adults who eat whole grains seem to be less prone to heart problems – they have less incidence of metabolic syndrome (a cluster of symptoms that make heart attack, stroke and diabetes more likely) and are less likely to die of cardiovascular disease. Look for amaranth, barley, buckwheat, bulgur, corn (including popcorn), millet, quinoa, rice, rye, oats, sorghum, teff, triticale, wheat and wild rice.

877

Love fruit and vegetables

Research at Dumfries and Galloway Royal Infirmary suggests eating plenty of fruit and vegetables may raise levels of salicylic acid (the key ingredient in aspirin, prescribed to people at high risk of heart attack). Plant sterols also seem to lower cholesterol levels significantly. A large European study found men who eat foods rich in lycopene (such as tomatoes) reduced risk of heart attack by half. Garlic helps lower cholesterol and blood pressure and makes arteries more elastic.

Mix your favourite fruits into fruit salads to help keep your heart healthy.

878
Porridge please

Eating porridge for breakfast can lower cholesterol levels, suggest studies, and keeps you feeling full enough to resist heart-unfriendly mid-morning snacks. Add potassium-rich chopped banana, which helps lower blood pressure.

879
Eat more magnesium

A diet rich in magnesium sources – whole grains, cashew nuts, avocado, spinach, halibut, tofu – protects against metabolic syndrome, suggests one study. Combine with food rich in omega-3 fatty acids, which work to support healthy cholesterol levels and reduce blood pressure.

880
Seeds and meat

Eating peanuts, walnuts and almonds correlates with lower cholesterol levels (people on peanut-rich diets also experience dips in triglyceride levels: high levels are associated with heart disease). Keep a bag of nuts and seeds in your desk drawer or sprinkle them on cereal. However, occasionally swap these plant proteins for meat because research suggests this can help keep blood pressure at healthy levels.

881
Good fat

Omega-3 oils may offer protection from coronary heart disease, though a recent review of multiple studies in the *British Medical Journal* didn't find a clear effect. Choose dietary sources over fish-oil supplements, which may be contaminated with heavy metals and carcinogenic man-made chemicals. Opt for small oily fish, hemp and linseed (flax) oils, argan oil and lingonberries. Grass-fed meat and organic cheese are also good. Avoid margarine: it may contain artery-clogging trans fat.

882
Chuck out salt

Reducing your salt intake by a third could cut your risk of heart disease by up to 40 per cent states the UK's Department of Health. The easiest way to control salt intake is to avoid processed food: salt lurks in the most unlikely places, including breakfast cereals, bread and biscuits.

883
Make fruit salad

Mix berries with chopped banana, apricots, nectarines, melon and figs. Fruit salad keeps the heart healthy by raising potassium levels, which helps keep blood pressure in check and so reduces the risk of stroke. Fruit fibre is good for healthy cholesterol. Finally, slug in some pomegranate juice: a recent study suggests it boosts arterial function.

884
Savour fine chocolate

Cocoa contains antioxidant ingredients that relax the blood vessels, promote circulation and reduce blood pressure. Make hot chocolate with cocoa powder or choose dark chocolate with 70 per cent cocoa solids.

885
Drink milk

A French study found that men who eat a good amount of dairy produce were less likely to develop metabolic syndrome, perhaps because calcium helps regulate blood pressure. Another study found dairy reduced risk of high blood pressure by half. Go for skimmed or semi-skimmed milk and low-fat yogurt because high-fat products have been linked with heightened risk of cardiovascular disease.

886
Drink wine

A glass of red wine a day is heart-friendly thanks to its antioxidant properties (which prevent artery hardening), and is associated with lower blood pressure and reduced stress levels.

Good digestion

If your digestive system isn't working well, you won't absorb all the youth-preserving nutrients you need from food. Keep digestion at optimum levels by building your diet around whole grains and fresh fruit and vegetables and make sure you are drinking plenty of water. Take time to enjoy your meals – enjoyment is key to good digestion.

Boost your friendly bacteria with a daily dose of probiotic yogurt.

887
Stop stressing
Digestion can become less effective if you feel anxious. Whenever stress takes over, stop what you're doing, close your eyes, empty your brain and focus on the even flow in and out of your breath. Let this prevent other thoughts from taking over.

888
Sit down to eat
Allow enough time for eating; sit at a table, and don't do anything else while you dine. Really enjoy everything you put in your mouth, savouring taste and texture.

889
When emotions play a part
If you are aware of a link between digestive symptoms and your emotions, consider hypnotherapy. Research suggests this is one of the most effective treatments for any form of irritable bowel syndrome.

890
Try herbal teas
Drink a cup of camomile, fennel, nettle or peppermint tea after a meal to aid digestion.

891
Top homeopathic heartburn remedies
Take these remedies up to three times daily while symptoms are present or for up to two weeks:
- Try Carbo.Veg 30c for heartburn accompanied by much burping.
- Nux.Vom 30c helps after eating spicy food or drinking alcohol.
- Take Robinia 30c for heartburn at night after lying down.

892
Top homeopathic constipation remedies
- Take alumina 30c, for constipation resulting from dryness in the bowel.
- Try Nux.Vom 30c, for frequent ineffectual urging.
- Use opium 30c, when there is no urge to go at all or the bowels are completely inactive.

893
Probiotic yogurt
Start the day with a helping of live natural yogurt to introduce healthy bacteria into your digestive system.

894
Yoga therapy
To extend the front of the body maximizing blood flow to the digestive system and make space for the internal organs try the yoga pose Supta virasana (see No. 753).

895
Digestive juice
Blend a small fresh pineapple with an apple, pear and stick of celery to create a breakfast juice that benefits the digestive system.

Keeping a clear head

Headaches seem to decline in number as the years pass. However, that doesn't mean we always have a clear head. Natural remedies can be effective – but before trying these, make sure you are not dehydrated by drinking water or eat a snack in case you are experiencing a blood-sugar dip. If symptoms are severe seek medical attention.

896
Stay focused
When concentration starts to fail, place 3 drops essential oil of basil or rosemary on a handkerchief. Inhale when you need to stay focused. (Avoid rosemary oil if you have epilepsy.)

897
Balancing the brain
To improve focus by enhancing right/left brain function, stand with feet hip-width apart. Raise your right knee and touch it with your left hand, then raise the left knee and touch it with your right hand. Repeat at least 20 times to feel a little brighter.

898
Top homeopathic headache remedies
Take these remedies up to three times daily while symptoms are present or for up to two weeks. Stop as soon as you start to feel better or after a week if it has not helped:
• Take Belladonna 30c, for throbbing headaches with a sensation of pressure in the head, when any movement makes the pain worse.
• Try Lachesis 30c, for pre-menstrual bursting/splitting headaches, or a headache accompanying a menopausal hot flush.
• Use Kali-Bich 30c, for headaches caused by sinusitis where most of the pain is felt in the forehead or cheeks.

899
Top homeopathic migraine remedies
• Iris 30c is used for neuralgic frontal headaches, often left-sided with nausea and blurred vision.
• Nat.Mur 30c is for headaches preceded by visual disturbances (often lightning zig-zags before the eyes) and followed by sickness.
• Sanguinaria 30c is best for bilious migraines that settle over the right eye and cause nausea and vomiting.

900
From head to toe
The reflex points for the brain and senses are in the toes and so rubbing your toes well and keeping them flexible can help clear the mind and decongest sinuses.

901
Eat chillies
At the onset of a sinus headache, make a salsa with finely chopped hot chillies, onion, tomato, coriander leaves and lime juice. Have a good helping to promote blood flow to the sinuses and assist mucus secretions. (A shot of chilli-infused vodka also works well.)

Chillies and coriander can treat sinus headaches.

Book a soothing massage to reduce built-up tension in the head, neck and shoulders.

902

Soothing massage

Head pain may result from tension in the neck and shoulders. The relaxation brought on by a massage, given by someone else, can help. Send your partner on a massage day school or book an appointment with a massage therapist at times of stress.

903

Pain-relieving essential oils

Some essential oils, including lavender, seem to reduce stress triggered by pain. In one study, people who inhaled essential oil of lavender while experiencing pain recalled less discomfort later, and seemed to suffer less anxiety. Place a drop on your pillow or a handkerchief.

904

Lavender therapy

Rub a drop of essential oil of lavender around the temples and exert pressure on them with index fingers to relieve headaches.

905

Relaxing with eyes covered

Place firm bolsters beneath your back and head to support your body from the lower back up. Make sure your head stays slightly higher. Wrap a narrow scarf around your eyes.

Lie back over the support, legs apart, feet dropping outward. **Check through your body** for tension. Let go of your jaw and mouth, and feel as if your face is without expression. Rest for 10–20 minutes. When coming out, remove the scarf but keep the eyes closed for a few moments.

906

Camomile soother

Camomile tea can sooth a stress headache. For a sinus headache try ginger tea (see No. 141).

907

Identify triggers

To identify headache triggers, keep a journal. Record the time of day of onset, the ingredients of recent food and drink and likely stressors. Look for patterns and discuss them with your doctor, herbalist or homeopath.

908

Chew leaves

Chewing one leaf of the common hedgerow herb feverfew (*Tanacetum parthenium*) daily is a traditional migraine preventative. During an attack, take 5–10 drops of feverfew tincture in water every 30 minutes to ease constriction of the cerebral blood vessels (often the cause of pain). (Avoid if taking blood-thinning medication, such as aspirin.)

What menopause?

Falling levels of the hormone oestrogen can lead to distressing symptoms, from hot flushes to depression and tiredness. Hormonal changes can begin years before the average age of the menopause, currently 48. Yoga can be especially beneficial in beating symptoms.

909
Don't diet

If you're trying to lose weight, don't diet. When you stop the diet and return to your regular eating habits, the pounds will return. Instead, change your diet for life by building it around whole grains, fish, fruit and vegetables, nuts and legumes. Don't see any foods as forbidden – have a little of what you fancy now and then, and compensate for it by taking more exercise or eating healthy food the next day.

910
Herbal help

The herb *Agnus castus* can relieve menopausal symptoms, including hot flushes, irregular menstruation,

Eating healthily helps your body cope with symptoms that can accompany the menopause.

depression, forgetfulness and high blood pressure. It acts on the pituitary gland to regulate hormone function and can be helpful after a hysterectomy. Take 10–20 drops of the tincture in water daily during the second half of the menstrual cycle.

911

Homeopathic remedy

Sepia is the mostly commonly used menopausal homeopathic remedy. It addresses "stagnant water", which means it can relieve symptoms such as hot flushes, poor circulation, headaches, heavy or painful menstruation and mental confusion. Take Sepia 30c daily for short periods while symptoms persist.

912

Visit a homeopath

Constitutional health is a very individual thing: no two people exhibit symptoms of any condition in quite the same way. This is why homeopaths ask many and detailed questions when selecting an appropriate constitutional remedy for a patient. Book a consultation for remedies to match your changing constitution.

913

Flower remedies

The Australian Bush Flower Essence She Oak is a great hormonal and emotional balance for those going through any hormonal transition, from puberty to the menopause. Take 7 drops morning and evening. It has a reputation for enhancing fertility, so take no chances while using it!

914

Supta baddha konasana

This stress-relieving pose can be of help when everything seems overwhelming. Add firm pillows or folded blankets until your back feels well-supported. Remain in the pose for as long as feels comfortable.

1 Take a pillow and place a small folded blanket or cushion on one end. Sit in front of the other end and place the soles of your feet together, letting the knees relax. If the groin is not comfortable, support your knees.

2 Lie back, with your head supported on the blanket or cushion, and take your arms out to the sides, palms facing up. With your eyes open or closed, breathe deeply into your abdomen and relax.

915

Find relief with yoga

Follow the sequence of poses set out here and opposite, specially devised to ease you through many of the symptoms of the menopause, especially if you can manage a daily practice. These are all suitable for complete beginners. If you are experiencing unusual difficulties contact a yoga therapist.

Dandasana pose – especially helpful before and during the menopause.

916

Leg raising

Lie on your back, side on and a short leg's length from a sofa or chair. Place a belt or long scarf around the foot closest to the support and raise your leg to vertical. Stretch your leg out onto the sofa or chair and relax for a couple of minutes in an easy stretch. Repeat to the other side.

917

Upavista konasana

Sit with legs wide apart and place bolsters between them. Rest forward with your abdomen supported, adding or removing support for comfort. To come out, inhale and raise the trunk carefully. Bring your legs slowly back together.

918

Dandasana

Sit upright on the floor with legs extended in front of you. Try to make your ankles and big toes touch. Press the backs of your legs onto the floor. Take your hands to the floor by your hips and lift your chest. To improve core stability, imagine zipping up a tight pair of trousers. Hold for a minute, breathing, and repeat three times.

Janu sirsasana: press through the heel to keep the leg long and straight.

919
Janu sirsasana

From Dandasana (see No. 918), bend your left foot in to touch the top of your inner right thigh; let the knee relax to the ground. Place your hands on either side of your leg and tiptoe your fingers forward. Keep length on the front of your body rather than forcing the head down. As you move forward, soften the area between your shoulder blades and don't "hunch" your back. Keep the abdomen soft. Inhale to come back to Dandasana, then repeat on the other leg.

920
Cooling relaxation

During heated, stressful moments, subside into relaxation with an eye bandage (see No. 905), a cooling pose beneficial during the menopause. Before you lie back, place an extra folded heavy blanket across your upper thighs and lower abdomen as a comforting weight.

921
Avoid excess pounds

Weight gain is a common problem around the time of the menopause. In one study, strength training twice a week for 15 weeks helped women significantly reduce abdominal fat and add lean muscle – and they didn't diet!

922
Destress now

A number of studies link stress in the 30s with a more difficult menopause (stress seems to disturb hormone balance). Adopt stress-reducing strategies that work for you (see Nos. 707–25) before the menopause kicks in for a more seamless transition.

923
Eat phytoestrogens

Phytoestrogens, oestrogen-mimicking plant nutrients, have a weak oestrogen-like effect in the body, and may raise falling hormone levels. In one study, women on a six-week phytoestrogen-rich diet reported decreased menopausal symptoms. Food sources include chick peas, lentils, alfalfa sprouts, soy beans or soy milk, and linseed (flax). (Consult your doctor if taking oestrogen replacement therapy.)

924
Anti-perspiration body mist

Keep this cooling misting spray in the refrigerator and spray liberally when you feel hot and bothered.

3 drops essential oil of cypress
2 drops each essential oil of coriander and bergamot (FCF grade)
1 tsp sweet almond oil

Drop the essential oils into the almond oil. Stir into a cup of water in a pump-action spray. Shake well before use.

925
Beauty oils

If skin is playing up, look for beauty preparations that include skin-balancing essential oils of camomile, rose and sandalwood. Add the same oils to bath-oil blends, too.

926
Skincare tricks

Squeeze a capsule of evening primrose oil nightly into facial oil blends: this oil provides building blocks essential for making sex hormones and may be effective in preventing hot flushes. Look for body lotions containing plant nutrients that resemble the hormone progesterone. REN's Wild Yam Omega & Body Repair Cream includes plant sterols from soybean extract and West African wild yam in a rich "clean" cream that helps skin retain a velvety moisture all day.

927
Cook with sage

Throw sage leaves into poultry and pork dishes, pumpkin and squash gratins, savoury apple sauces and use to garnish green beans. This

herb is a mild plant oestrogen, recommended by herbalists to counter menopausal hot flushes and night sweats.

928
Look forward not back

As we get older, it is easy to get into the habit of dwelling on lost opportunities. However, after the menopause many women experience renewed vigour and zest for life, and go on to found businesses, climb mountains, run marathons or write novels.

929
Focus on freedom

The menopause is a time of loss but it is also a time of liberty. When symptoms get you down, ponder the positive aspects of being free from the pull of female hormones.

930
Yoga breathing

Alternate nostril breathing can be very helpful in calming and cooling. Follow the instructions for rebalancing breath – see No. 320.

931

Sage tea recipe

Cultivate a few sage plants in the garden or in a pot by the kitchen door and pick fresh to make this tea. A few sprigs of mint (Moroccan for preference) enhance the flavour.

- 1 tbsp fresh sage leaves
- sprigs of mint, optional
- half a fresh lemon
- honey, to taste

1 Remove twigs and discoloured leaves then place the sage leaves and mint sprigs (if using) into a teapot. Pour over boiled water and steep for 10–20 minutes (place a tea cosy over the pot).

2 Strain the tea into a cup to remove the leaves. Add a squeeze of lemon and some honey to taste, if you like tea sweetened a little. For best flavour, drink while the tea is hot.

Healthy prostate

For men, being aware of natural ways to look after the prostate gland becomes more important as the decades pass. You can do this by eating the right foods and practising yoga. Consult your doctor if you experience symptoms including urination abnormalities or lower back pain.

932
Herbal aid
To reduce benign inflammation of the prostate and relieve a range of troublesome urinary symptoms, try taking a combination of the herbs saw palmetto (*Serenoa serrulata*), hydrangea (*Hydrangea arborescens*) and horsetail (*Equisetum arvense*) – take up to 30 drops of the combined herbal tincture in water daily.

933
Cook with linseed oil
Make salad dressings with linseed (flax) oil, and use it also as a moisturizer over areas of dry skin.

Drink pomegranate juice to counter prostate cancer.

US research suggests this oil may slow the growth of prostate tumours when used as part of a low-fat diet.

934
Max on minerals
Research shows that men with low selenium levels are more likely to develop prostate cancer. Boost selenium levels by eating seeds and nuts every day. Research demonstrates that eating zinc-rich pumpkin seeds could reduce inflammation of the prostate gland.

935
Drink pomegranate juice
In one study, pomegranate extract seemed to slow the growth of prostate cancer. Have a glass of pomegranate juice for breakfast.

936
Enjoy a little sun
Research suggests that exposure to UV rays can protect men from prostate cancer and delay its onset by an average of five years. The key factor is vitamin D, created during exposure to the sun.

937
Chilli cure
In tests with mice, chillies seemed to cause suicide in prostate cancer cells. Use them in fresh salsas and curries, and infuse in olive oil and vodka.

938
Ketchup time
Lycopene, found in tomatoes, is protective for the prostate. Cooked tomato products contain more useful amounts than fresh.

939
Yoga posture to boost prostate health
Sit upright with the back of your pelvis touching a wall. If this feels difficult sit on a yoga block or firm cushion (achieving the correct angle on the back helps open the groin).
Stretch your legs in front of you and take them as wide apart as you can. Bend your legs until the soles of the feet press together and the knees drop out to the sides.
Rest the backs of your hands on your thighs, elbows and shoulders relaxed, chest lifting. Close your eyes and breathe. To come out, bring your knees together, wrap your arms around them and squeeze gently.

Protecting bones

From the mid-30s, women begin to lose bone mineral density, causing bones to become brittle – a condition known as osteoporosis. There are proven ways to reverse this age-related loss: increasing calcium intake is one, and daily weight-bearing exercise is another.

940

Take weight-bearing exercise

Bone-mineral density was shown in one American study to be best protected by weight-bearing exercises such as dancing, trampolining, walking, skipping and aerobics.

941

Arm and wrist strengthener

To strengthen the arms and wrists, start in Downward dog (see No. 530). Stretch into your heels and firm the legs. Keeping the arms straight, move your head and shoulders forward until your shoulders are over your wrists. Your body should be rigid, like a plank, with no sags and curves. Spread the hands well and maintain the stretch down the legs and into the heels. Take a couple of breaths and move back into Downward dog, then rest with bottom on heels. Repeat two or three times.

942

Simple strong standing

Stand with feet together, heels, big toes and ankles touching. Spread your toes. Press down with your heels and lift your knee caps. Roll the inner part of the groin back. Engage your lower abdominal muscles (imagine zipping up a tight pair of jeans). Lengthen the sides of the waist, lift your breast bone, broaden your collar bones and relax your shoulders. Extend the back of the neck. Standing tall and firm, breathe. Practise this posture when you have to stand for long periods, and when waiting in line or at the water cooler.

943

Tree balance

To strengthen the legs and ankles and bring confident balance, start in simple strong standing. Ground your feet (see No. 372).

Keeping your left leg really firm, raise the right foot a little off the ground. Lift it higher (using hands if necessary), placing the sole as far up your inner left leg as you can. Press the foot and the leg towards each other.

Take weight-bearing exercise to help preserve bone-mineral density.

To prevent wobbles, fix your gaze on an object or place one hand against a support. When you feel secure, stretch one or both arms overhead. The more you stretch, the easier the pose. Breathe. Come out of the pose slowly and under control and repeat the moves with the other leg.

944
Homeopathic health

Try the tissue salts Calc.Phos, Calc. Fluor and Silica to help maintain healthy bones. These low potency homeopathic remedies can be safely taken over several months to prevent or reduce osteoporosis. They work by correcting minor deficiencies in these essential salts, supplying them in an easily assimilated form. Take two tablets up to four times daily.

Boost calcium absorption with bok choi and broccoli.

945
Nurturing friends

Having a close circle of friends to rely on seems to protect older women from thinning of the bones and other age-related ailments, including Alzheimer's, heart disease, rheumatoid arthritis and even cancer, by controlling levels of an inflammatory protein, suggests a recent American study. Try to arrange to spend a night out with girlfriends every week.

946
Start a garden

For older women, gardening can be as effective at building bones as gym-based weights work – and even more effective than jogging, suggests an American study in *Journal of Women and Ageing*. For best results

Physical activity such as gardening can be effective at building bones.

make sure your gardening includes some carrying, squatting, pushing and digging.

947
Walk with sticks

Nordic walking (using poles to work the arms and upper body) is said by practitioners to engage 90 per cent of skeletal muscles. Running uses 70; swimming a mere 35. Enrol in a class to learn the technique and hook up with a group of enthusiasts.

948
Broccoli for bones

Broccoli and bok choi are some of the few greens that promote absorption of calcium, strengthening bones. Use in soups and stir-fries.

949
Change to brown rice

Calcium requires magnesium as well as vitamin D for maximum absorption. In a study reported in the *Journal of the American Geriatrics Society*, people over 70 who consumed highest levels of magnesium had greater bone-mineral density than people with the least amount of this mineral. Brown rice contains more than half as much again per serving than white rice. Other good sources include cashew nuts, salmon, soybeans, tofu and oats.

950
Drink tea

Long-term tea drinking may improve bone mineral density. Black tea or green tea both seem to be effective. If you prefer herbal, choose nettle tea, which is full of bone-essential nutrients.

951
Soak up some sun

Vitamin D is essential for calcium uptake. To generate vitamin D, especially in winter or if you have darker skin, aim to sit in the sun (unprotected by sunscreen) for 10–15 minutes daily. As you get older this becomes more important: studies suggest the epidermis and dermis levels of older skin are less able to synthesize the vitamin from UV rays.

Banishing backache

Back pain affects about two thirds of adults in the UK, but thankfully it doesn't seem to worsen with age. Physiotherapists blame modern lifestyles: slumping on the sofa, badly contoured office chairs, obesity and stress. One of the best ways to prevent back pain is to exercise most days and pay attention to good posture basics (see Nos. 305–18).

952
Back rub

Try this blend of oils after a sports session or a long day at work.

4 tbsp sunflower oil
8 drops essential oil of lavender
4 drops essential oil of juniper
2 drops essential oil of peppermint

Pour the sunflower oil into a clean, dark glass bottle, drop in the essential oils. Lid and store in a cool, dark place. Shake before use.

953
Top homeopathic back pain remedies

For a painful back, take one of these remedies up to three times daily while symptoms are present or for up to two weeks. Stop when your back is better or after a week if it has not helped.
• Hypericum 30c eases back pain following a spinal injury.
• Kali.Carb 30c relieves lower back pain around the sacral area.

• Rhus Tox 30c, helps a back that "seizes up" after a period of inactivity, but eases with movement.

954
Leg and arm lifting

To strengthen the back, lie on your front with arms extended above your head, forehead on the floor. On an inhalation lift a body part; on an exhalation release it to the floor. Follow this sequence: right arm, left arm, right leg, left leg, right arm and right leg, left arm and left leg, right arm and left leg, left arm and right leg, both arms, both legs, both arms and both legs together three times.

955
Supported back arch

To relieve fatigue in the upper back, fold a rolled blanket lengthways and place on the floor. Lie with your back over the blanket (level with your heart). Take your arms apart, palms up. Relax for a few minutes as the back steadily releases. Breathe.

956
Supported bridge pose
To remove tension from the lower back, assemble two or three yoga blocks and a folded blanket. Lie on your back with knees bent, feet flat on the floor. Raise your hips high and slide as many of the supports under your pelvis as you can, soft layer on top. Relax your bottom onto the support, the whole of the sacrum and pelvis supported and lower back free. Lie back, spread your arms and enjoy.

957
Yoga release
For relief from back pain, try the passive twist (No. 847), or follow tip No. 361, but support your upper body on a cushion.

958
Pressure points
Work on pressure points on the feet can help relieve back pain. In one study, older people treated by a reflexologist had a 60 per cent reduction in symptoms of back, hip and knee pain.

959
Quick reflexology fix
If you can reach your feet, massage the inner arch and heel, and across the ball of the foot and big toe.

960
Find a chiropractor
Chiropractors treat the musculo-skeletal system, working largely on the spine to treat the nervous system and promote self-healing.

961
Time for a new mattress?
If your mattress is more than eight years old it may be time for a new one. Choose an organic mattress to cut exposure to toxins, and make sure you air it daily and turn it once a month (over and end to end).

962
Heat the back
Applying a heat wrap to the lower back when it is in pain seems to get workers back to work more quickly than doing nothing suggests research. Improvise by lying on a hot water bottle wrapped in a towel.

963
Talking to God
Over 30s with spiritual beliefs are better at coping with chronic illness than those without, suggests research from Johns Hopkins University.

Reflexology treatments work on pressure points on the feet to help relieve back pain.

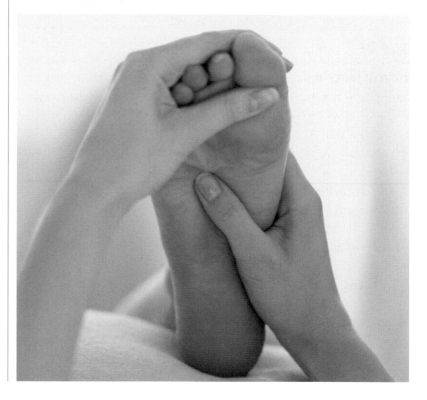

Keeping joints moving

Most people over 60 suffer from osteoarthritis to some extent. When joints start to stiffen, the range of movement available to them every day decreases, which leads to yet more stiffness. Exercise is a key way to keep joints loose; weight control helps too. Make sure exercise sessions include cardio, weight work and stretching.

Visit your homeopath for advice on remedies to relieve joint pain.

964
Destress

Rheumatoid arthritis is an auto-immune disease that causes painful flare ups of inflammation. Sufferers tend to have higher levels of stress. Use all the stress-busting tips on pages 144–46.

965
Have a love-in

Research shows that people who fight or are depressed or stressed, tend to have raised levels of inflammatory proteins in the blood: high levels may make arthritis, cardiovascular disease and certain cancers more likely. In one study, people with small injuries healed more quickly if they stayed on good terms with ex-lovers.

966
Get spiritual

A study of people with rheumatoid arthritis at Duke University Medical School in North Carolina found joint pain was reduced, mood heightened and support more likely when patients recorded spiritual thoughts in a daily diary. Set up a meditation diary to express your day-to-day spiritual feelings. They don't have to be profound or informed; simple appreciation of your life is enough concluded the study.

967
Top homeopathic joint pain remedies

For joint pain, take up to three times daily while symptoms are present or for up to two weeks. Stop as soon as you start to feel better or after a week if it has not helped:
- Arnica 30c is for pain or inflammation of the joints caused by injury or overwork.
- Ledum 30c is for joint pain that becomes worse when the body is overheated (for example, in bed), or for joints that feel cold.
- Rhus Tox 30c is for joint pain resulting from cold, damp weather.

968
Herbal help

The herb devil's claw (*Harpagophytum procumbens*) has strong anti-inflammatory and pain-relieving effects on the joints, and is commonly used by those who suffer from osteo- and rheumatoid arthritis as well as by people who experienced chronic muscular pain. You might like to try it in cream or supplement form, using as instructed on the pack. (Avoid if you have peptic ulcers.)

969
Learn t'ai chi

Korean research suggests learning t'ai chi for 12 weeks can ease some of the pain associated with osteoarthritis. Women who attended classes reported reduced pain, better balance and more ease of movement in their daily activities. Look for t'ai chi for arthritis programmes; these are popular in Australia.

970

Yoga with a partner – front thigh stretch

One person relaxes face down on the floor, legs outstretched, arms, neck and head comfortable. The partner carefully picks up the right foot and gently presses it towards the buttocks, stretching the front thigh. Work slowly and sensitively to avoid putting pressure on the lower back. Hold for two minutes, then do the second leg. Swap over. This can be amazingly effective and relaxing, releasing tension in the thighs.

971

Yoga with a partner – leg raising

One person stands with his or her back to a wall. Bending the knees (not the back), the second person catches the right heel and lifts the leg until the standing partner feels a comfortable stretch and the standing leg stays firm. Extremity of stretch won't help mobility; being able to maintain the stretch long enough for the body to accept the movement is more important. Now do the other leg. Swap over.

972

Keep exercising

Resistance and strength-training exercises seem to aid people who suffer from rheumatoid arthritis and leg/hip osteoarthritis, helping reduce pain and promote the strength and flexibility to keep everyday movements intact. Persevere with this form of exercise, even if you find walking and weight-bearing difficult: weight-training rebuilds muscle mass that can be lost through inflammation and treatment with corticosteroids.

973

Flank stretch

This pose helps maintain mobility in the hips and lower back as you get older and more stiff. You might like to also try the Downward dog pose: follow the instructions in tip No. 530.

1 Lie on your back with knees bent and feet flat on the floor. Place your right ankle on your left thigh, just above the knee. (If you find this exercise difficult, place a scarf or belt behind the knee to help pull it towards your chest.)

2 Reach forward to catch the left knee (or pull on the ends of the scarf) and draw the knee towards your chest. Maintain control without straining the upper back and neck. Hold for a few breaths, then try the other side.

974
Eating by colour
Fill up on orange and red fruit and vegetables. They contain the carotenoid beta-cryptoxanthin, which may reduce risk of inflammatory polyarthritis (a precursor of rheumatoid arthritis) by up to 40 per cent according to a study reported in *American Journal of Clinical Nutrition*.

975
Consider supplements
Glucosamine sulphate supplements (from lobster and oyster shells) may stimulate cartilage building and offer significant reductions in pain and stiffness in osteoarthritis. Chondroitin supplements (from animal cartilage) are thought to inhibit cartilage breakdown, reducing pain and improving joint function. However, a recent study found no clear evidence of the benefits of these supplements.

976
Avoid red meat
Red meat may aggravate inflammation so if you have rheumatoid arthritis eat no more than once a week. Substitute small oily fish and walnuts. Not only do omega-3 fatty acids reduce risk of heart attack, lower blood cholesterol, improve mood and raise immunity,

Bay leaves are effective in relieving aching joints and have an analgesic effect.

they have anti-inflammatory properties. Studies suggest they might ease joint pain when taken with glucosamine sulphate.

977
Try MSM
Try topical creams containing MSM (methlysulfonylmethane), an organic derivative of sulphur. Some claim it reduces the formation of free radicals. In a study of people with osteoarthritis those taking MSM supplements reported reduced joint pain and aches after exercise. MSM is also available as a bath bomb.

978
Journal it out
In a study reported in the *Journal of the American Medical Association*, arthritis patients who spent three 20-minute sessions writing about stressful events reported a 28 per cent reduction in symptoms even four months later. A control group

who wrote on a neutral topic saw no improvement. Don't feel you need to write stress out every day: even occasional journaling has therapeutic effects.

979
Bay leaf joint soak
Relaxing in herb-flecked water for 12 minutes helps soothe away aches and pains.

6 tbsp bay leaves
6 tbsp dried marjoram
12 tbsp sea salt

Whizz the herbs in a coffee grinder to a smooth paste. Stir into the salt and dissolve in a bowl with double the amount of hot water. Swish into a very warm bath as the tap is running. If your feet and ankles are painful, halve these quantities and use in a footbath.

980
Ginger bath
Two thirds of a group taking ginger for osteoarthritis in a University of Miami School of Medicine study reported improvements in pain, stiffness and mobility. To soak in a ginger bath, grate 5cm (2in) fresh ginger root into the centre of a piece of muslin. Tie the ends together to secure. Suspend with string beneath the hot tap while filling a very warm bath, then cast in to soak. Spend at least 20 minutes in the bath.

Boosting immunity

As we become older, our immune systems become less effective, putting us at greater risk of infection, especially from newly circulating bacteria and viruses. The best way to enhance immunity seems to be to eat foods rich in nutrients and take light exercise most days. If you feel your immunity is compromised, visit a homeopath.

Raw garlic has antiviral properties.

981
Try transcendental

In a study into Transcendental Meditation (TM), those practising had less than half the number of doctor's visits and days in hospital than a closely matched control group. TM is always taught face to face. Search online for a class or ask your doctor for a referral.

982
Wrap up well

When you go out in cold, wet weather, wear the right clothes. In a study, students who immersed their feet in cold water for 20 minutes were more likely than those who didn't to come down with a cold 4–5 days later.

983
Acting quickly

When you feel a cold coming on, take a couple of doses of the homeopathic remedy Aconite 30c;

this may prevent further symptoms from developing. If a cold is making its entrance with much sneezing and watery mucus, try Nat.Mur 30c in the evening and again next morning to stop it in its tracks.

984
Look after your family

If your partner is ill, you are more likely to suffer bad health, suggests research from Harvard Medical School (those whose partners had a debilitating illness were more likely to die early). Nurse each other through minor illnesses so you both remain in good health and can benefit from two incomes for longer.

985
Sleeping matters

Getting only four hours' sleep a night for six nights has been shown to weaken the immune system. In a University of Chicago study, students who did so had levels of protective antibodies lower than

those who got eight hours' kip. If you regularly burn the candle at both ends, have a lifestyle rethink.

986
Fresh produce

Buy or grow carrots, spinach and broccoli, sweet potatoes, pumpkins, tomatoes and apricots. Plant sterols in these foods seem to help the body fight infection by increasing the number of T-cells (white blood cells that play a large role in the body's defence system).

987
Brew ginger tea

To diminish cold symptoms, grate 5cm (2in) fresh ginger root into a pan and cover with 4 cups of water. Bring to the boil and simmer, covered, for 10 minutes. Strain into a cup, squeeze in the juice of half a lemon and sweeten to taste with local honey. Drink as required through the day.

988
Eat garlic

As soon as you feel symptoms of a cold, add two raw cloves of garlic a day to food for its antiviral properties: grate onto toast with olive oil and fresh tomato, add to salad dressings, or stir into pasta before serving. Use until symptoms subside. Use fresh garlic in cooking through the year to strengthen the body's defences against viruses.

989
Try echinacea

Purple coneflower (*Echinacea purpurea*) has been clinically demonstrated to stimulate the production of white blood cells and is well known for its antimicrobial action. Take 30 drops daily of the tincture in water, or take capsules as directed on the pack to treat any kind of infection. It is particularly effective for upper respiratory infections and skin diseases (apply as a poultice). (Don't take for more than four weeks without a break.)

990
Good combination

Astragalus membranaceus (huang qi or milk vetch) is less well known than echinacea but equally effective. A tincture made from its root is a great lymphatic cleanser, and also acts as an energy tonic (take 30 drops daily in water). Accompany with ginseng tea for a month or so in the autumn to set you up for a winter free of coughs and colds.

991
Wash out your nose!

Neti pots are used in yoga practice for *jala neti*, nasal washing. This can help keep the airways clear and prevent chronic catarrh and rhinitis. Using a neti pot (Google it) or small sterilized teapot, dissolve 1 tsp salt in 600ml (1 pint) tepid water. Tilt your head sideways over a sink. Placing the spout of your pot against one nostril, pour the saline solution up your nose. The stream of water should trickle and then pour out of the other nostril. Blow your nose well, then repeat on the other side. If this is uncomfortable or your nose feels sore, reduce the amount of salt.

992
Yoga for the overtired

Yoga practitioners find immunity is lowered when we become overtired. Passive postures are beneficial: practise passive twists and backbends (see Nos. 847 and 849), Supta virasana (see No. 753), Supta baddha konasana (see No. 914), relaxation and breathing exercises. When you feel less tired, support all your body systems by practising any of the other yoga postures in this book or by going to a yoga class and keeping mobile and strong.

Herbal healing with echinacea helps stimulate white blood cell production.

993
Drink probiotics

Chuck back a shot of probiotic bacteria daily in a yogurt drink: a Swedish study shows that this can cut incidence of sick leave.

994
Make chicken soup

Chicken soup speeds recovery from cold symptoms such as sneezing and coughs.

roasted chicken carcass
1 litre (1¾ pints) chicken stock
bouquet garni
carrot, roughly chopped
onion, peeled and quartered
celery stick, roughly chopped
salt and freshly ground black pepper
handful fresh parsley, chopped

Cut away breast meat from carcass and reserve. Place carcass in heavy pan and cover with stock. Add bouquet garni, carrot, onion and celery, and simmer covered for one hour. Remove carcass and herbs and strain. Add breast meat, season and cook for a further 15 minutes. Stir in chopped parsley just before serving.

995
Extreme vitamin C

Vitamin C seems to work best as a preventative for days of physical exertion outdoors in cold weather, suggests one study. To power wound healing, artery health and collagen production as well as immunity, include several food sources in your diet daily. Choose from kiwi, mango, papaya, melon, blackcurrants, strawberries, raspberries, citrus fruit, tomatoes and rosehip tea.

996
Drink more green tea

Sip green tea daily for its powerfully antioxidant effects. Studies suggest it promotes immunity and can help ward off colds.

997
Burn tea tree

In a room vaporizer add 3–4 drops essential oil of tea tree to destroy circulating airborne germs.

998
Garnish meals

Add chopped fresh coriander leaves to salads and salsas, curries and grills. They have an antibacterial action shown in trials to be effective even against the food poisoning bug *Salmonella choleraesuis.*

999
Wash your hands

Viruses are most often picked up by touching infected surfaces (doorknobs, computer mouse, telephone), then transferred to the mouth, nose or eyes. To reduce your risk, wash your hands frequently during the day, and especially before eating.

1000
Natural antiseptic spray

Add 15 drops of essential oil of lavender to half a cup of water, then decant into a spray-pump bottle. Spritz surfaces to eliminate bugs and bacteria twice a day.

1001
Be happy

Happy people not only tend to be less susceptible to illness; when they do succumb, they recover more speedily. Think positive to enhance your immune function, zap stress, and keep yourself independent in later life.

Strawberries supply vitamin C to power health and immunity.

Resources

For details of stockists, mail order and treatments at approved salons, spas and department stores:

Burt's Bees
www.burtsbees.com

Caudalie
www.caudalie.com

Decléor
www.decleor.co.uk

Dr Hauschka
www.drhauschka.com

Elemis
(inc Visible Brilliance facial)
www.elemis.com

Green People
www.greenpeople.co.uk

Jurlique
(inc Rejuvanessence facial)
www.jurlique.com

Lavera
www.lavera.co.uk
www.lavera-usa.com

Living Nature
www.livingnature.com

Organic Make-up Company
www.organicmakeup.ca

The Organic Pharmacy
www.theorganicpharmacy.com

Primavera
www.primaveralife.com

REN
www.renskincare.com

Spiezia Organics
www.spieziaorganics.com

Weleda
www.weleda.com

Yin Yang Joint Bombs/
MSM Cream
www.yinyangskincare.com
www.gandgvitamins.com

Green cleaning products
www.seventhgeneration.com
www.ecoverproducts.co.uk

Index

About the author

Susannah Marriott is a freelance writer who specialises in complementary healthcare. She is the author of 12 illustrated books on yoga, spa treatments, meditation and prayer, and natural approaches to pregnancy and motherhood, including *Total Meditation, Basic Yoga, Spice Spa, The Art of the Bath* and *Your Non-Toxic Pregnancy.* Her writing has appeared in *Weekend Guardian* and *The Times, Zest, Shape, Top Sante, Healthy, She* and *Junior*, and she has broadcast on BBC Radio 4. In her 40s, Susannah lives with her husband and three young daughters in Cornwall, where she lectures on writing at University College Falmouth. She spends her free time practising yoga, growing fruit and vegetables, and occasionally DJing.

Acknowledgments

Author's acknowledgments

Thanks to Penny for getting the ball rolling, Esther for being so enthusiastic and Carole and Angela for making everything fit so beautifully. Special thanks to Julia and Amanda for providing expert and concise advice at the drop of a hat. Also to Celeste Lutrario and Tricia Sabine for beauty expertise, Ross Jackson for hair styling and tips, Jenny Wells for sex tips and Penny McFarlane for thoughts on therapeutic writing. Most of all, thanks to Parker for recipes and keeping children, home and garden thriving while I write.

Contributors

Julia Linfoot BSc MCPH MARH is a Registered Homeopath and has been in practice in South London since 1999. She prescribes herbal tinctures, flower essences and tissue salts as well as homeopathic remedies. She supervises student homeopaths, and teaches workshops and short introductory courses in homeopathy and health.

Bellenden Therapies: tel: 0207 732 1417; email: juliahomeopath@btinternet.com

Amanda Brown has been teaching yoga for 17 years. She also practises as an artist and a natural therapist.
Tel: 01326 318776
email: magicbean_99@yahoo.co.uk

Publisher's acknowledgments

Dorling Kindersley would like to thank Ann Baggaley for proof-reading and Sue Bosanko for the index. They would also like to thank Ruth Jenkinson for the new photography, Carole Ash for photography art direction, Roishin Donaghy for hair and make-up and Liz Belton for styling. Thanks also to Fresh and Wild and Neals Yard.

Models: Suzi Conway and Francine Bloom from Close Agency; Melanie Searle and Amanda Grant from Model Plan Agency; Susannah Marriott.

Picture credits

The publisher would like to thank the following for their kind permission to reproduce their photographs:

(Key: a-above; b-below/bottom; c-centre; l-left; r-right; t-top)

Alamy Images: Richard Morrell 79tr. **Anthony Blake Photo Library**: Tim Hill 30bl; Sian Irvine 21tl; Maximilian Stock Ltd 170tr; Tony Robins 20bl. **Corbis**: 8tr; John Henley 179br; Michael Keller 54tr, 71; Larry Williams 31br. **Getty Images**: altrendo images 51br; Ross Anania 49; Roderick Chen 14bc; Ric Frazier 52tr; Jens Koenig 167; Antony Nagelmann 163tr; Lisa Romerein 146bl; Andrew Wakeford 138tr. **Jupiterimages**: Burke/Triolo Productions 173; Wally Eberhart 144b, 149br; Nonstock 133tr. **Masterfile**: Peter Griffith 180tr. **Photolibrary**: Botanica 162bl. **PunchStock**: BananaStock 17b, 53br, 87tr; BrandXPictures 27, 133cra, 151tr; Comstock 143tl, 148tc, 161bl; Corbis 60br; digitalvision 62tr; image 100 156tl; Imageshop 33; Imagesource 93bl, 121tc; Photodisc Red 50c, 56bl, 72tc, 89; Purestock 61tr; stockbyte 37tr.

All other images © Dorling Kindersley
For further information see:
www.dkimages.com